Capel Bond

Six Concertos, in Seven Parts,

for four violins, a tenor violin, a violoncello, with a thorough bass for the

harpsichord. N. B. The first is for a trumpet, the sixth a bassoon concerto

Capel Bond

Six Concertos, in Seven Parts,
for four violins, a tenor violin, a violoncello, with a thorough bass for the harpsichord. N. B. The first is for a trumpet, the sixth a bassoon concerto

ISBN/EAN: 9783337315627

Printed in Europe, USA, Canada, Australia, Japan

Cover: Foto ©Thomas Meinert / pixelio.de

More available books at **www.hansebooks.com**

SIX
CONCERTOS,

IN

SEVEN PARTS,

FOR

FOUR VIOLINS, a TENOR VIOLIN,

A

VIOLONCELLO,

With a THOROUGH BASS for the

HARPSICORD,

Compos'd by

CAPEL BOND,

ORGANIST of COVENTRY.

N. B. The Firſt is for a TRUMPET, the Sixth a BASSOON CONCERTO.

❊❖❊❖❊❖❊❖❊❖❊❖❊❖❊❖❊❖❊❖❊❖❊❖❊❖❊❖❊❖❊❖❊❖

Printed for the AUTHOR; and Sold by Mrs. JOHNSON, *Cheapſide*, LONDON, and by
Mr. BOND at COVENTRY.
MDCCLXVI.

SUBSCRIBERS

WORK.

A
The Rt. Hon. the Earl of Aylesford
John Afh, M. D. Birmingham
Mr. Avifon, Organift of Newcaftle upon Tyne
The Mufical Society at Afhby de la Zouch

B
Sir Henry Bridgman, Bart.
Henry Toy Bridgman of Princknafh, Efq; Glocefterfhire
Mifs Sally Bradbourn, Chefterton, Shropfhire
Colonel Bonham
Paul Baine, Efq;
George Birch, Efq;
James Birch, Junr. Efq;
Oldfield Bowles, Efq;
The Rev. Mr. Bree, Allefly
The Rev. Mr. Bridges
Mr. Richard Burford, Banbury
The Mufical Society, Ditto
Mr. Bacon of Clerkenwell, London
The Mufical Society, CherryOrchard, Birmingham
Mr. Brown, Organift of the Cathedral Church, Lichfield
Mr. Richard Burney of Worcefter
Mr. Balam, Organift, Walfall
Mr. Bond, Birmingham
Mr. Bond, Organift, Wolverhampton
The Mufical Subfcription Concert, Birmingham

C
The Right Hon. Lord Craven
Sir Thomas Cave, Bart.
Thomas Cave, Efq;
Mrs. Cave
—— Clevering, Efq; Northampton
Mifs Carver, Birmingham
Mr. Edward Carver, Ditto
Mr. Capper, Junr. Ditto
Mr. Clark, Organift of St. Philip's, Dit.
Mr. Cater, Coventry
The Mufical Society, Ditto
Mr. Chilcott, Organift, Bath
Mr. Clack, Organift, Hereford

D
The Rt. Hon. the Countefs of Denbigh
The Rt. Hon. the Earl of Donegall, 2 Sets
Mifs Dicey, Northampton
John Darker, Efq;
The Rev. Mr. Dovey, Birmingham
The Rev. Mr. Francis Dawes, Elmdon
The Rev. Mr. Darwell, Walfall

Mr. George Dundas, Banbury
Mr. Edward Davis, Organ Builder

E
The Rev. Dr. Edwards, D.D. Coventry
The Philharmonic Society at Ely

F
Mrs. Fraunces
The Rev. Mr Felton, Hereford
Mr. Franklin
Mr. William Ferry, Northampton

G
Sir Henry Gough, Bart.
Lady Gough
Mifs Grove, Coventry
William Grove, Junr. Efq; Ditto
Robert Grayham, Efq;
Mr. Gough, Perry Hall
Mr. Francis Goodwin, Banbury
Mr. John Gardnor, at his Academy, Kenfington
Mr. Anthony Greatorex, Organift of Leicefter

H
Sir Lifter Holt, Bart.
Sir Samuel Hellier, L. L. D.
Chriftopher Horton, Efq; Catton
Mifs Harris, Birmingham
The Rev. Mr. Hopkins, Copready
The Rev. Mr. Hughes, Radway
The Rev. Mr. Howlette, Bedworth
Doctor Hayes, Oxon
Mr. Philip Hayes, Efq;
Mr. Holden, Birmingham
Mr. Hobbs, Organift of St. Martin's, Ditto
Mr. Hobbs, Organift, Banbury
Mr. Higgins, London

I
Charles Jennens, Efq; 6 Sets
Palmer Johnfon, Efq;
Mr. Ifaac, Organift, Worcefter
Mr. Jones of Sudbury
Mrs. Johnfon, 6 Sets

K
Edward Knight, Junr. Efq; Wolverly
Mr Kirkman, Coventry
Mr. Kirkman, Harpficord Maker, Lon.

L
The Right Hon. Lord Leigh
The Hon. Mifs Leigh
Mifs Loyl'd
David Lewis, Efq;
Mr. Lates, Oxon
The Cicilian Society at Lichfield
The Mufical Society at Leicefter

M
Walter Acton Mofeley, Efq;
Mr. Millar, London

N
The Senr. Mufical Society at Nottingham

P
The Rt. Hon. the Earl of Plymouth
The Right Hon. Lord Piggott
Sir John Palmer, Bart.
Girton Peake, Efq; Birmingham
The Rev. Mr. Parker, Coventry
The Rev. Mr. Pixel
Mrs. Pixel
The Rev. Mr. Pepperrell
The Rev. Mr. George Palmer
Mr. John Lilly Parker, Merchant, Wolverhampton
Mr. Pemberton, Duddefton

R
Mr. Richards, Afhby de la Zouch
Mr. David Richards of Bath
Mr. Rook, Organift of All-Saints, Briftol

S
Sir Charles Shuckburgh, Bart.
Mrs. Scott, Woolfton
Mifs Spooner, Elmdon
Mifs Kitty Spooner, Ditto
Mr. Smith, Organift of the Cathedral Church, Glocefter
Thomas Swale, Efq;
Mr. Sawyer, Birmingham
Mr. Saville, Vicar, Choral of the Cathedral, Lichfield
The Mufical Society in Stourbridge, Worcefterfhire

T
John Tredway, Efq;
John Taylor, Efq; Birmingham
Mifs Twigg, Ditto
Mr. John Twigg, Junr. Ditto
Meff. Tafwell and Luntley

V
Mrs. Vane, Putney
Mr. John Valentine of Leicefter

W
The Hon. John Ward
Mrs. Williams, Glocefter
Will. Wickham, Efq; Swackliff, Oxon
Mr. Watts, Coventry
Mr. Henry Wolley, Northampton
The Mufical Society at Wolverhampton
The Mufical Society at Worcefter

VIOLINO PRIMO DEL CONCERTINO

Con Spirito

CONCERTO I

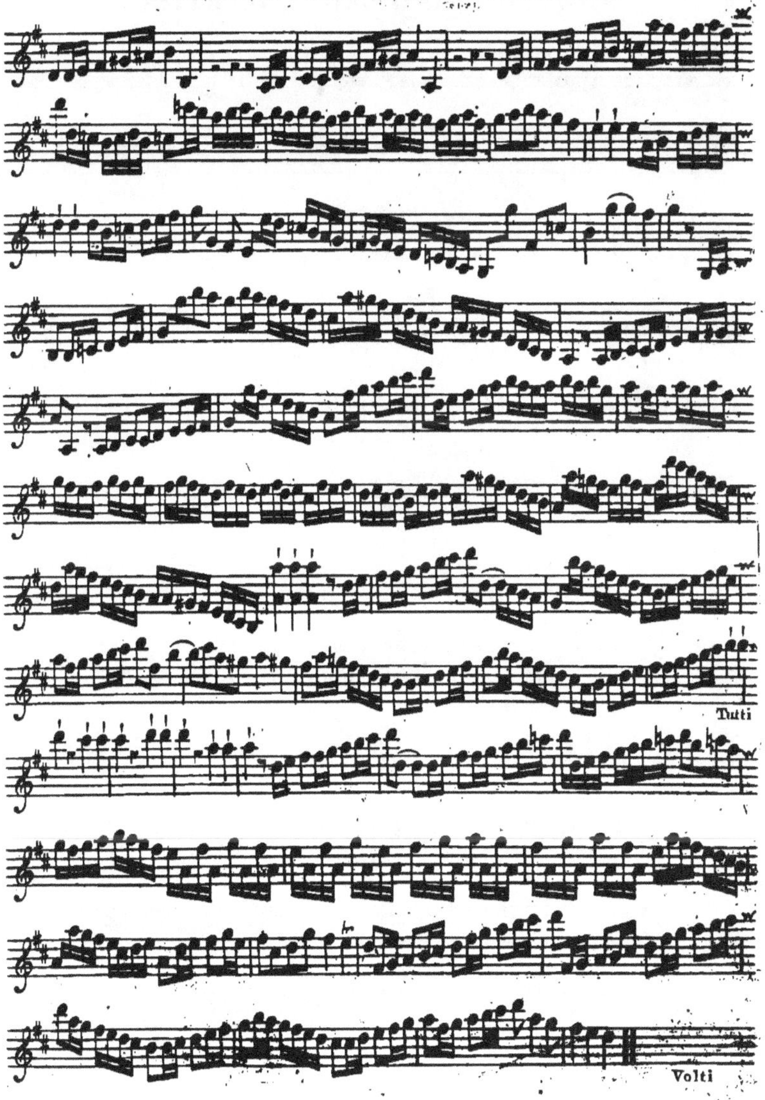
Tutti
Volti

Mezzo Pia
Larghetto
Tutti
Mezzo Pia
Tutti
Dolce Pia
Tutti Pia
Fortiss.o
CONCERTO II
Maestoso
P.
F.
P. Soli
Tutti P.
F.
P.
F.
P.
F.
P.

Al Tempo Giusto

Soli

Tutti

Adagio   Volti

VIOLINO PRIMO DEL CONCERTINO

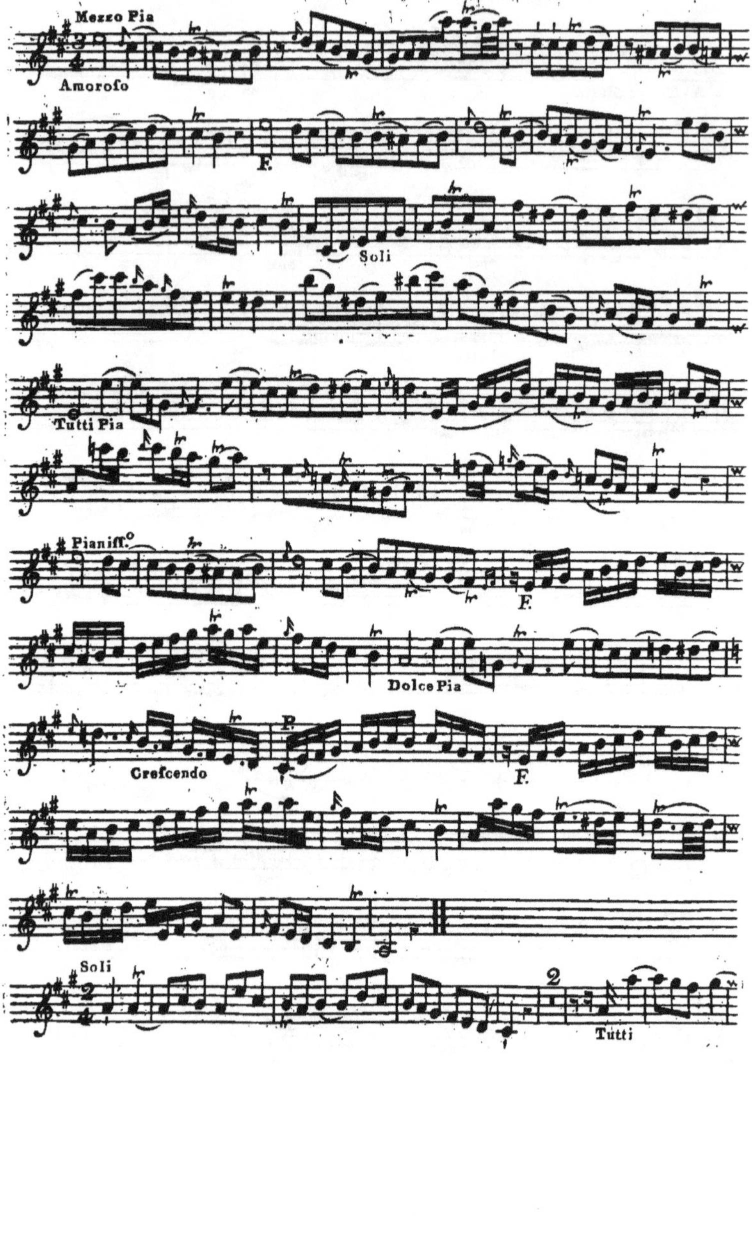

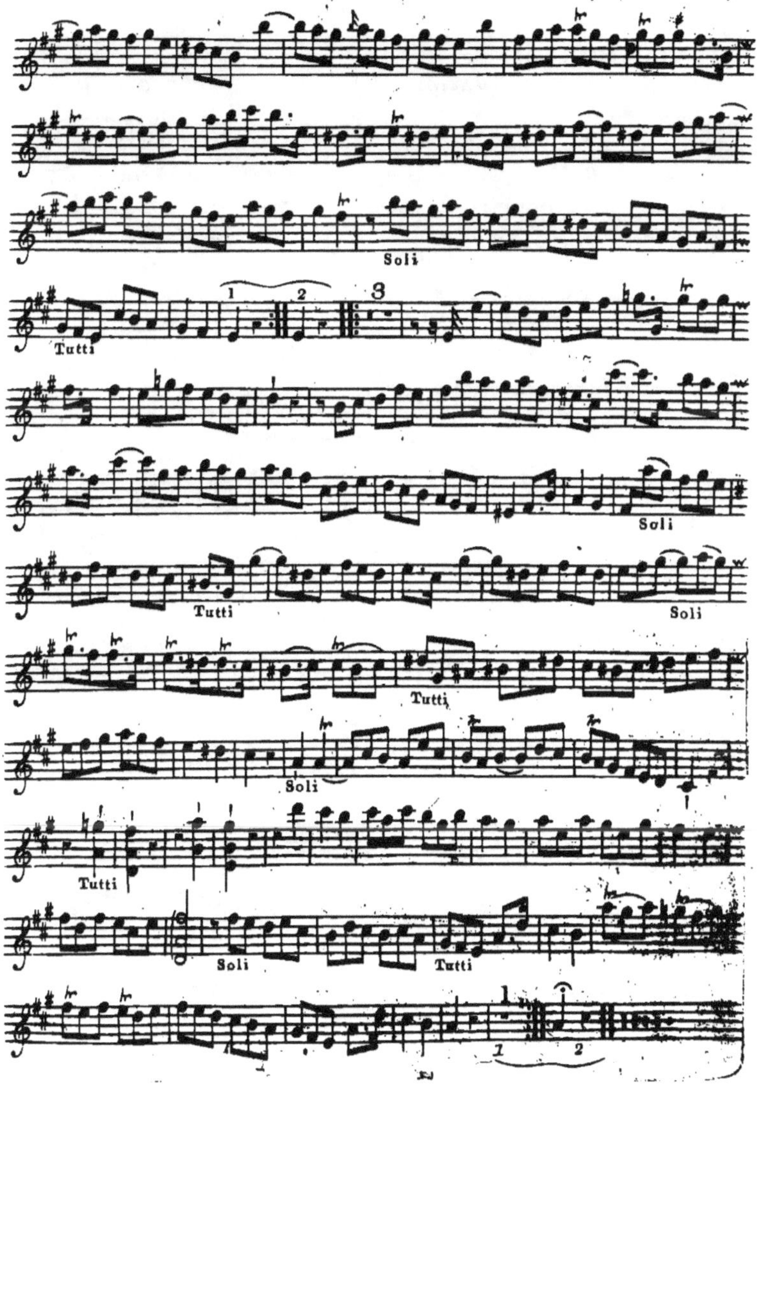
Soli
Tutti
Soli
Tutti
Soli
Tutti
Soli
Tutti
Soli
Tutti

CONCERTO III

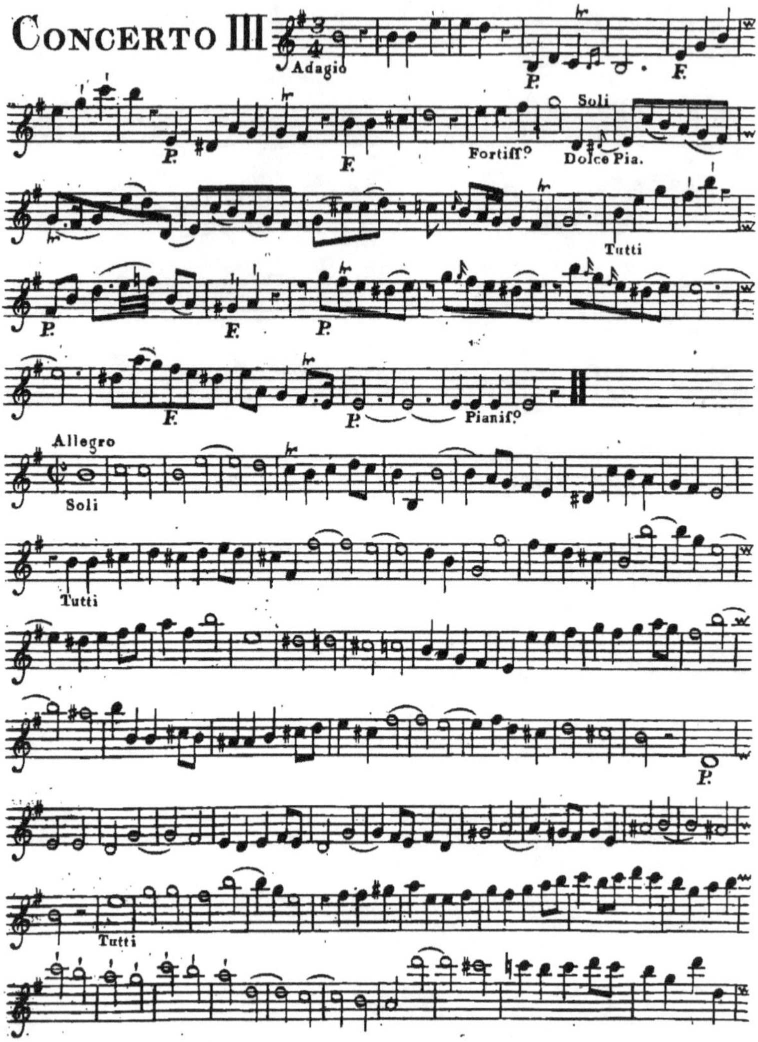

Soli
Tutti
Dolce Pia
Affettuofo
F.
P.
F.
Solo
Tutti
Solo
Dolce Pia
F.

CONCERTO IV

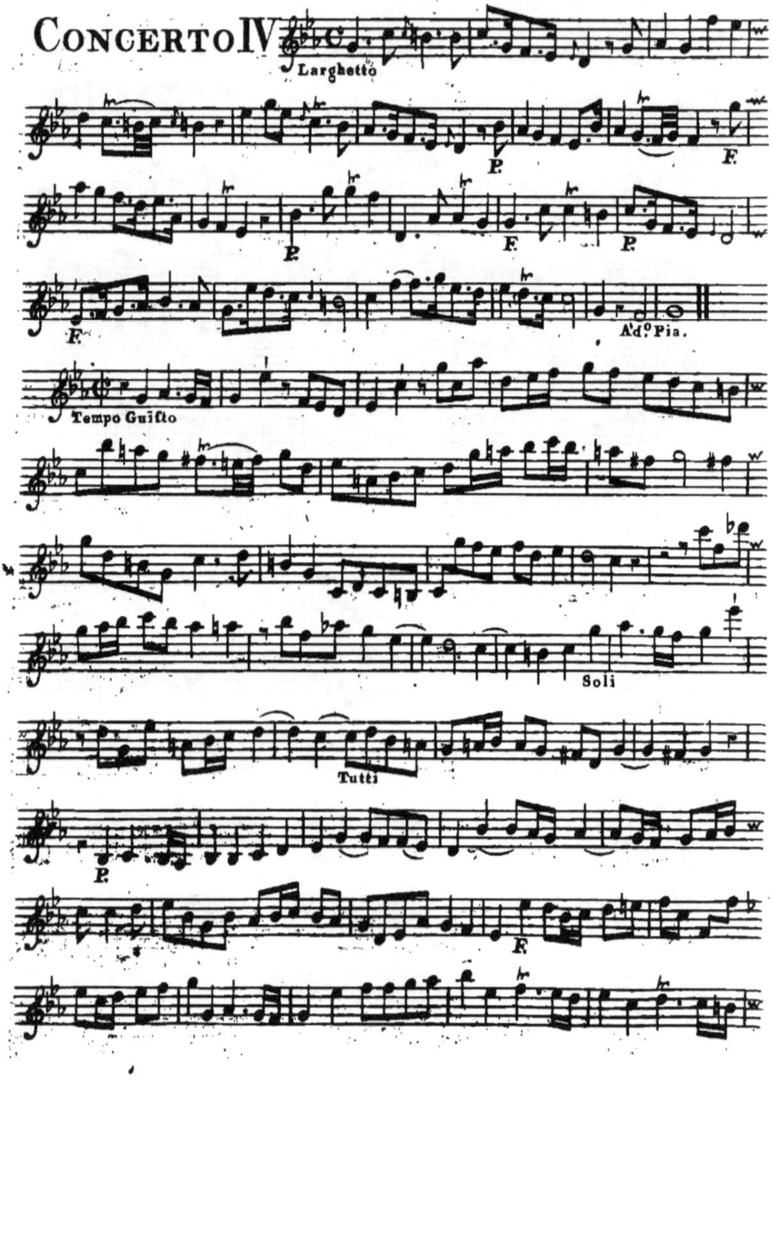

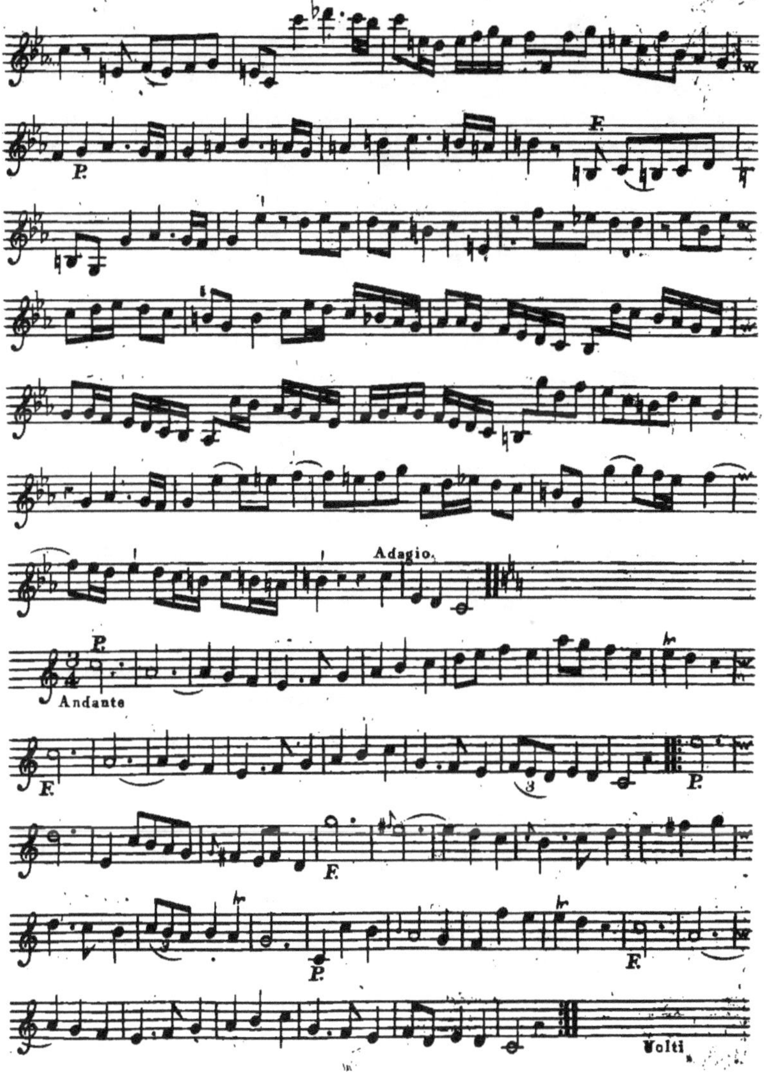
P.
F.
Adagio.
P.
Andante
F.
P.
F.
P.
F.
Volti

VIOLINO PRIMO DEL CONCERTINO

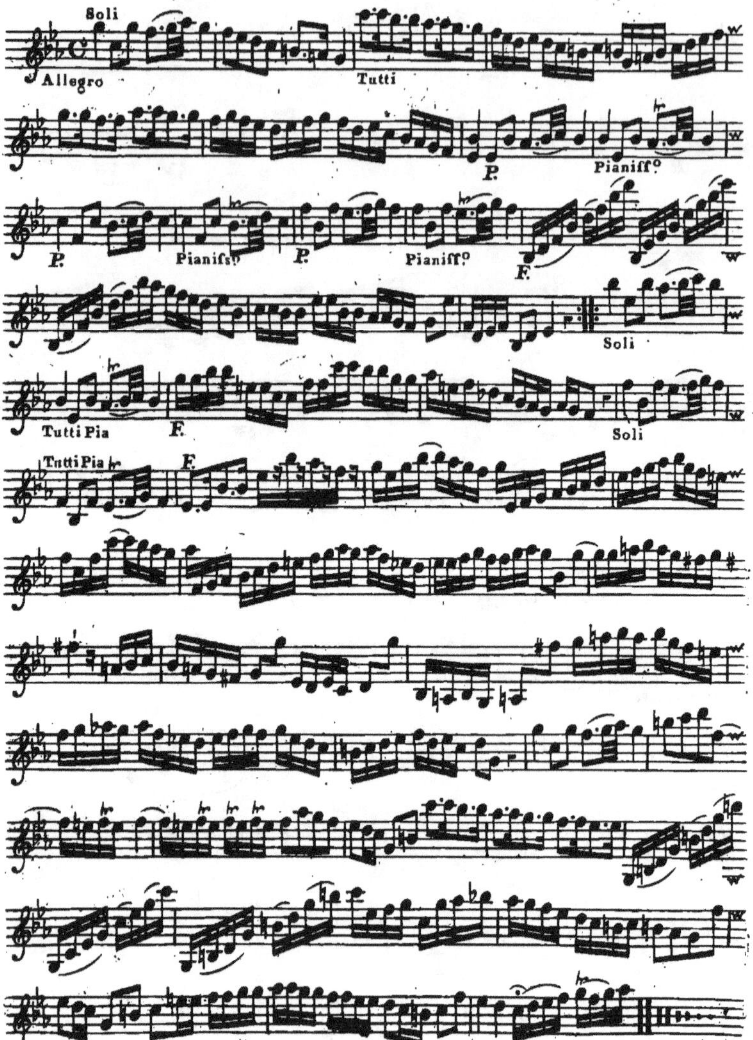

CONCERTO V

VIOLINO PRIMO DEL CONCERTINO

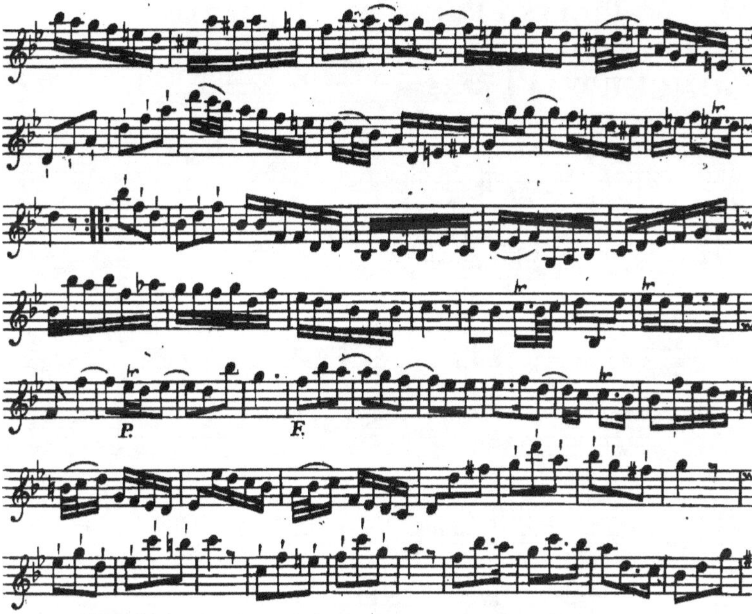
P.
F.

VIOLINO PRIMO DEL CONCERTINO

CONCERTO VI

Affettuoſo
P.
7
P.
Pianiſſ.o
Creſcendo
F.
6
Pia. Creſcendo
F.
P.
Allegro
18
F.
4
P.
15
F.

SIX
CONCERTOS,

IN

SEVEN PARTS,

FOR

FOUR VIOLINS, a TENOR VIOLIN,

A

VIOLONCELLO,

With a THOROUGH BASS for the

HARPSICORD,

Compos'd by

C A P E L   B O N D,

ORGANIST of COVENTRY.

N. B. The Firſt is for a TRUMPET, the Sixth a BASSOON CONCERTO.

.

✢✧✱✧

Printed for the Author; and Sold by Mrs. Johnson, *Cheapſide*, London, and by
Mr. Bond at Coventry.
MDCCLXVI.

CONCERTO I

Volti

Larghetto
Mezzo pia.
Tutti
P.
Tutti
Dolce Pia.
Tutti Pia.
Tutti Fortiss.

CONCERTO II

Maestoso
P.

F.
P.
F.
P.
F.
P.
F.
P.
Al Tempo Giusto
Soli
Tutti
2

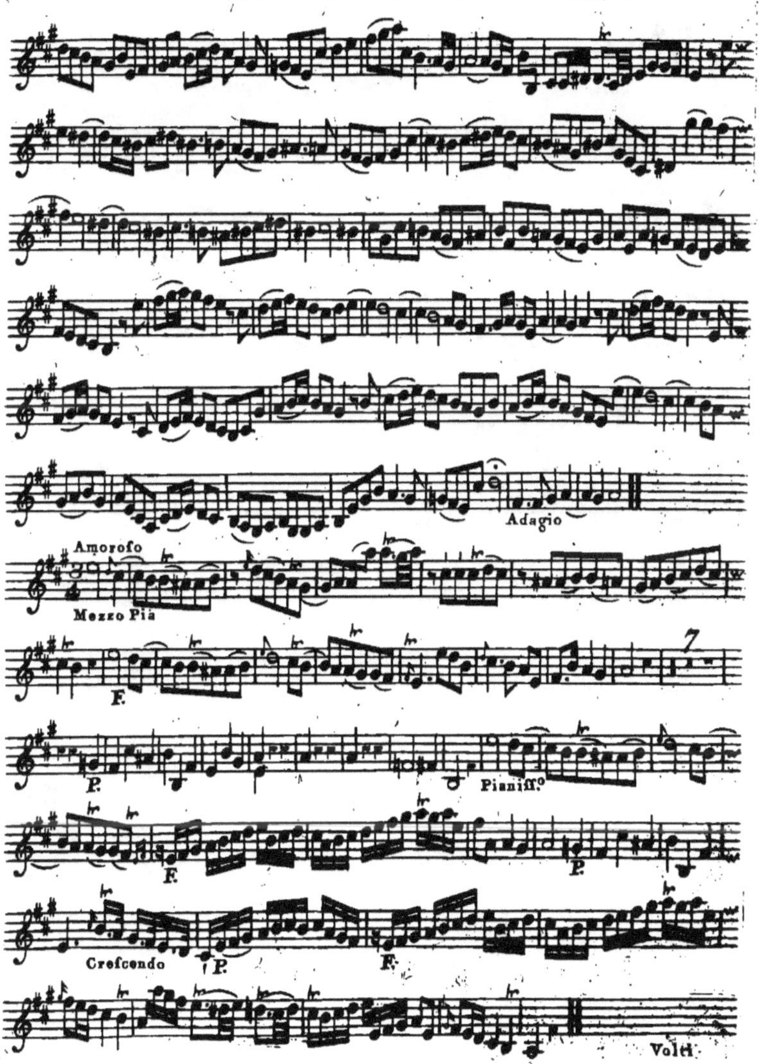
Adagio
Amorofo
Mezzo Pia
F.
P.
Pianiff.o
Crefcendo
Volti

VIOLINO SECONDO DEL CONCERTINO

CONCERTO III

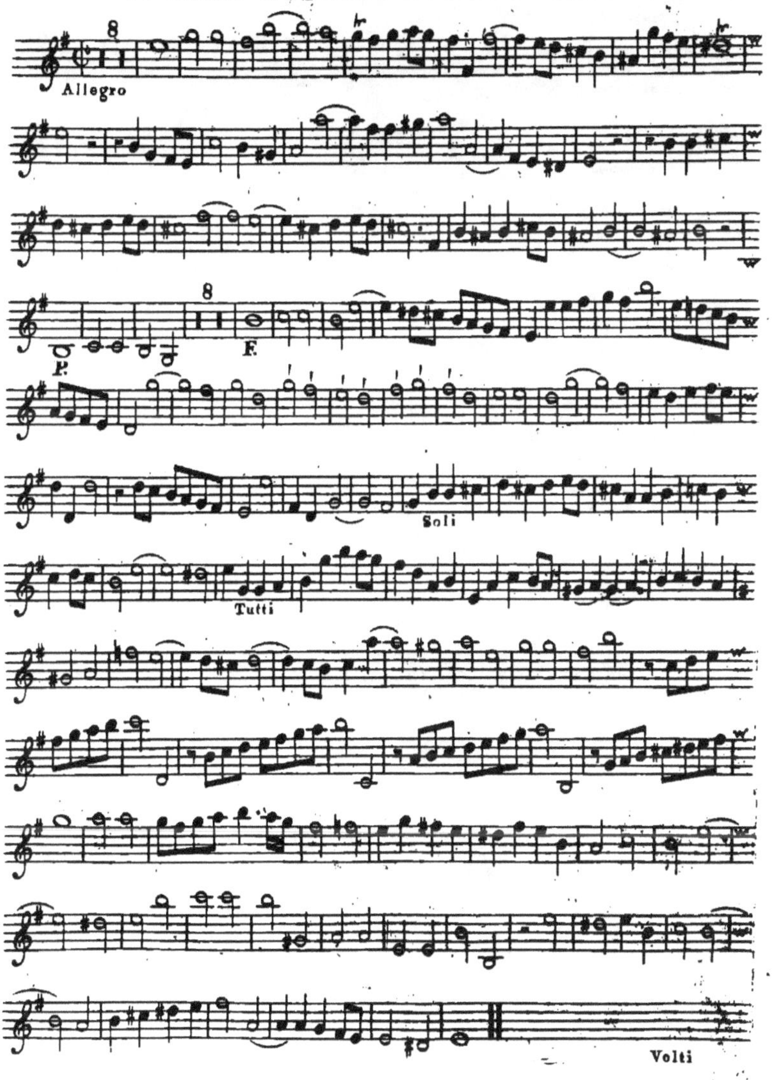
8
Allegro
P.
8
F.
Soli
Tutti
Volti

Affettuoso
Dolce Pia
F.
P.
F.
P.
Tutti
P.
Dolce Pia
F.
CONCERTO IV
Larghetto
P.
F.
P.
F.
P.
F.
Adº Pia.
Tempo Giusto

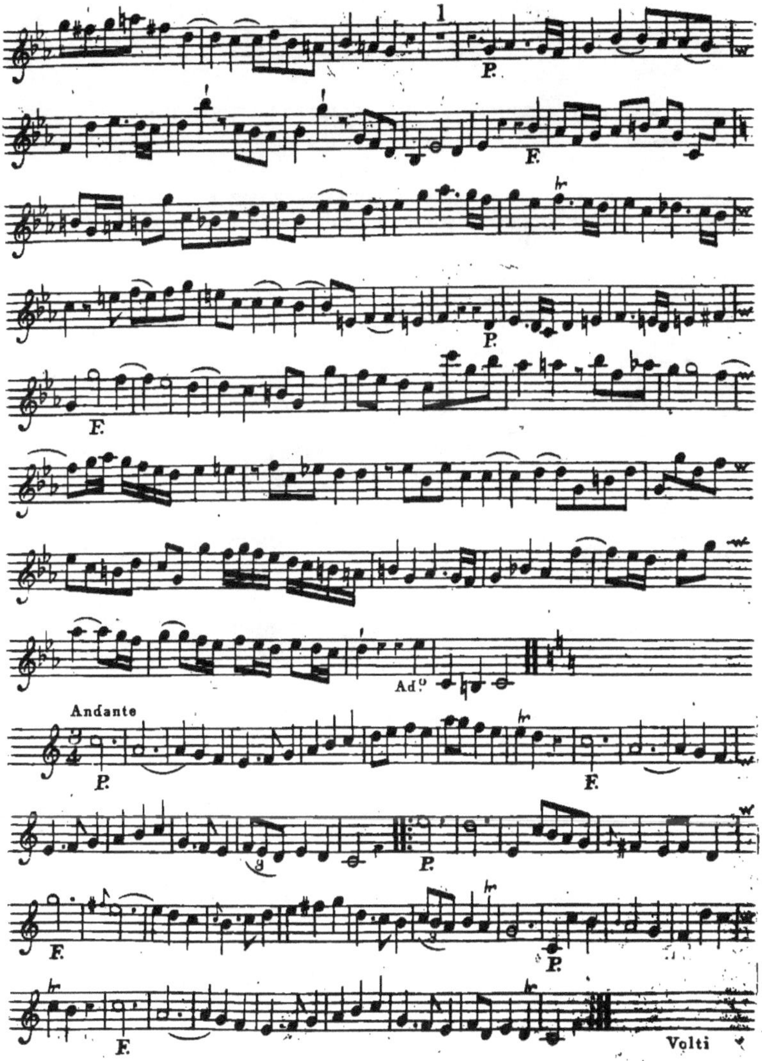
1
P.
F.
P.
F.
Ad.°
Andante
P.
F.
P.
F.
P.
F.
Volti

VIOLINO SECONDO DEL CONCERTINO

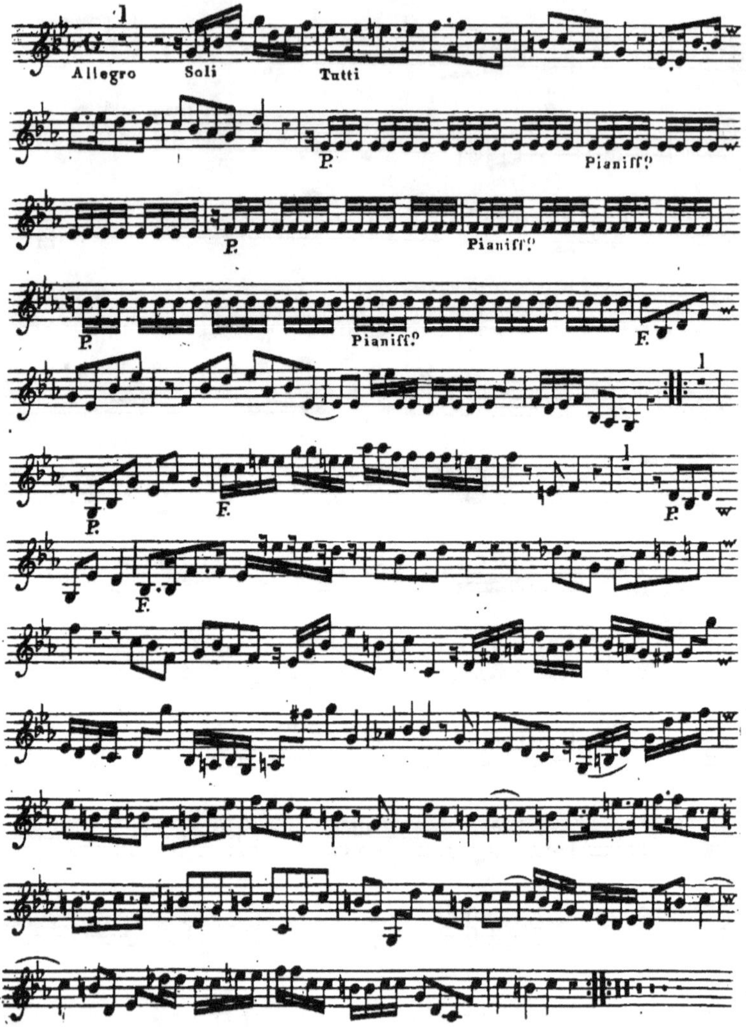

CONCERTO V

VIOLINO SECONDO DEL CONCERTINO

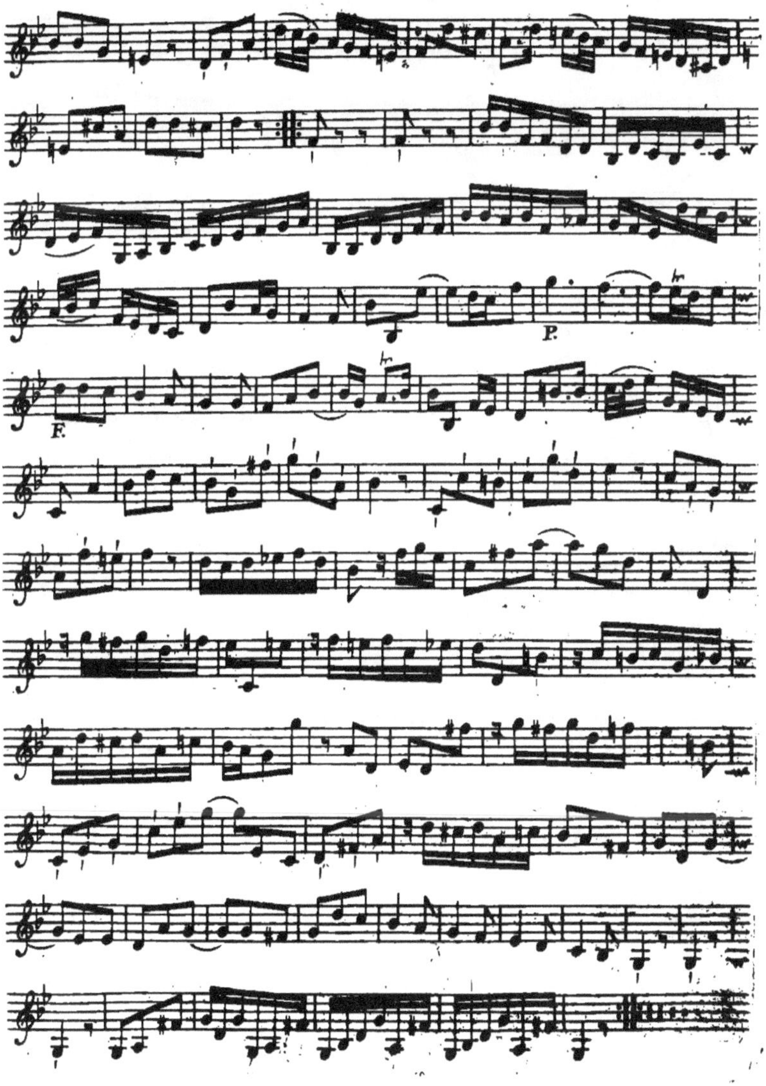
P.
F.

CONCERTO VI

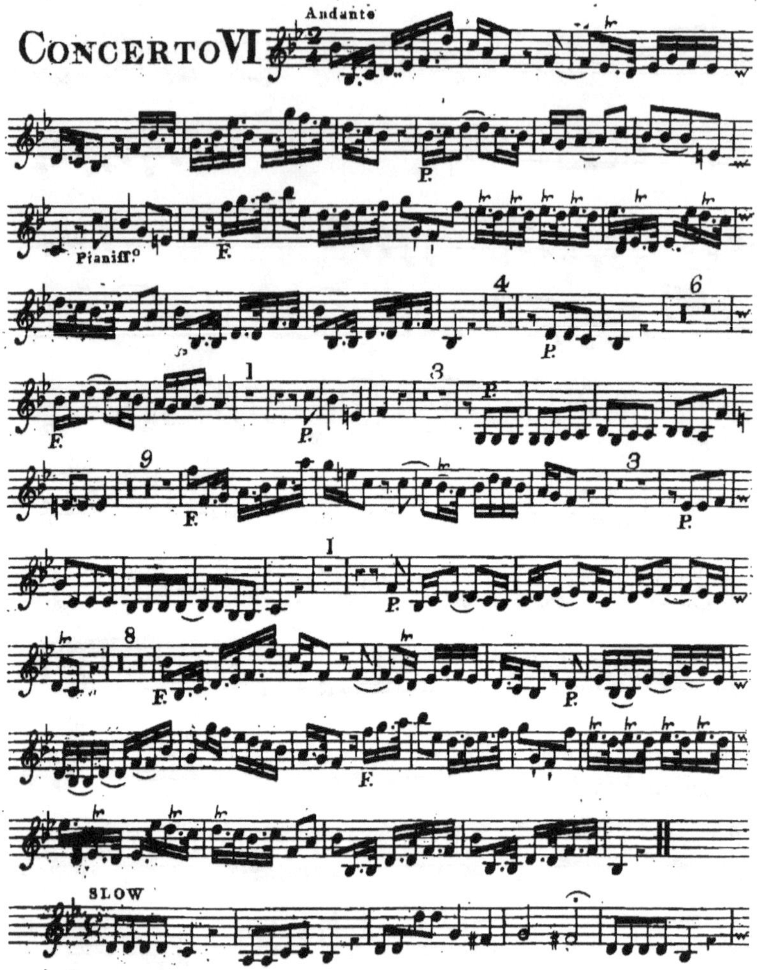

Affettuofo
P.
7
P.
Pianiff.°
Crefcendo
F.
6
Crefcendo
F.
P.
Allegro
18
F.
4
P.
15
F.

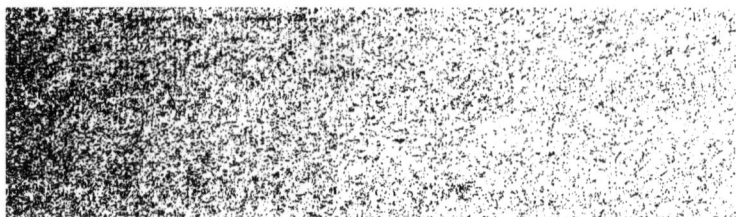

BASSOON

CONCERTO VI

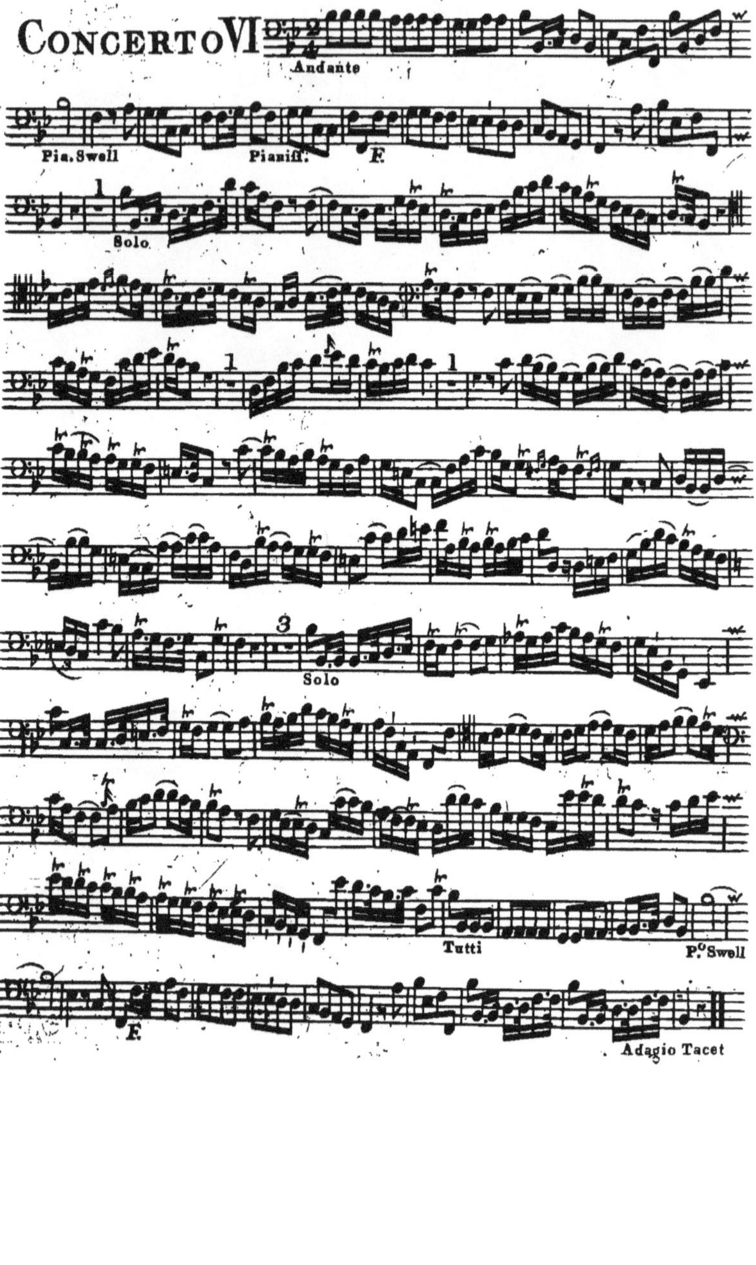

Bassoon

Solo
Affettuoso
Tutti Pia.
Tutti
P.
Allegro
Solo
Tutti
Solo
Tutti

TROMBA

CONCERTO I

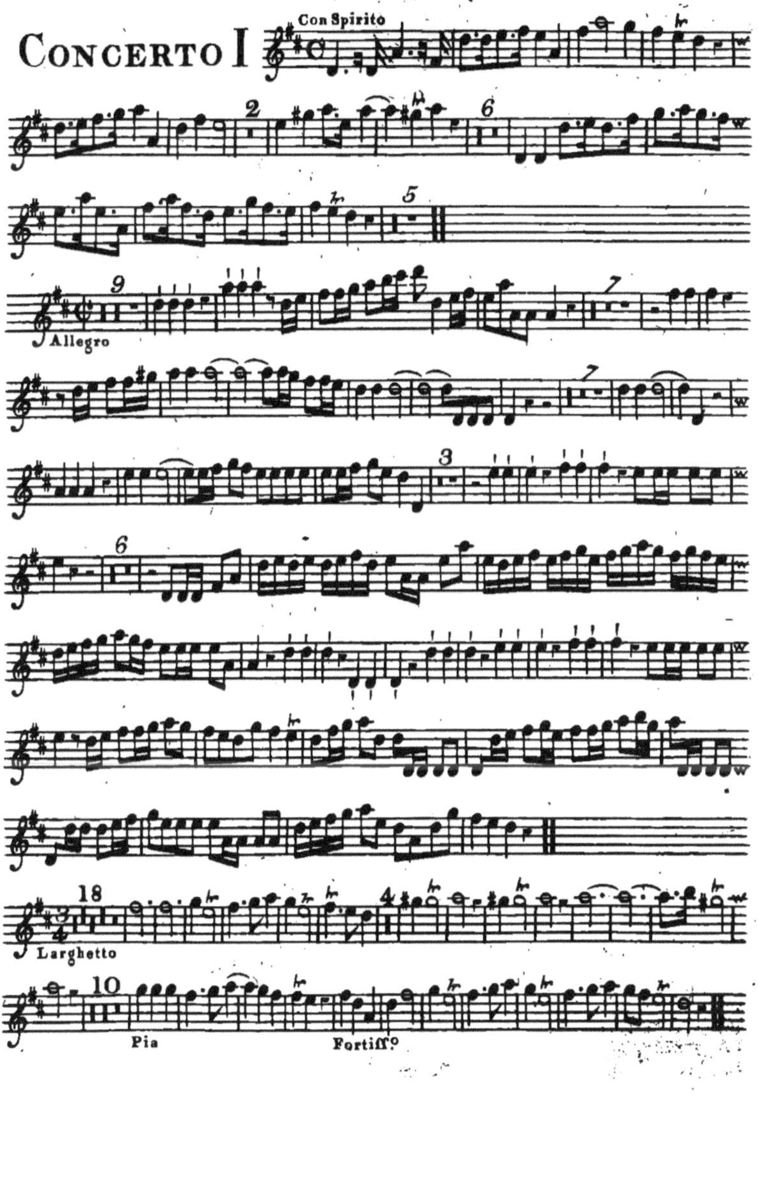

SIX
CONCERTOS,

IN

SEVEN PARTS,

FOR

FOUR VIOLINS, a TENOR VIOLIN,

A

VIOLONCELLO,

With a THOROUGH BASS for the

HARPSICORD,

Compos'd by

CAPEL BOND,

ORGANIST of COVENTRY.

N. B. The Firſt is for a TRUMPET, the Sixth a BASSOON CONCERTO.

•

Printed for the AUTHOR; and Sold by Mrs. JOHNSON, *Cheapſide*, LONDON, and by
Mr. BOND at COVENTRY.
MDCCLXVI.

Bond, Capel, d.1770.

VIOLINO SECONDO RIPIÉNO

CONCERTO I

Con Spirito

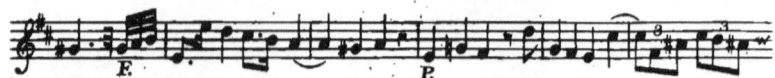

Dolce pia.

F.   P.

3   3   3   3

Pianiff.º

Adº Pia.

F.

Allegro

Violino Secondo Ripieno

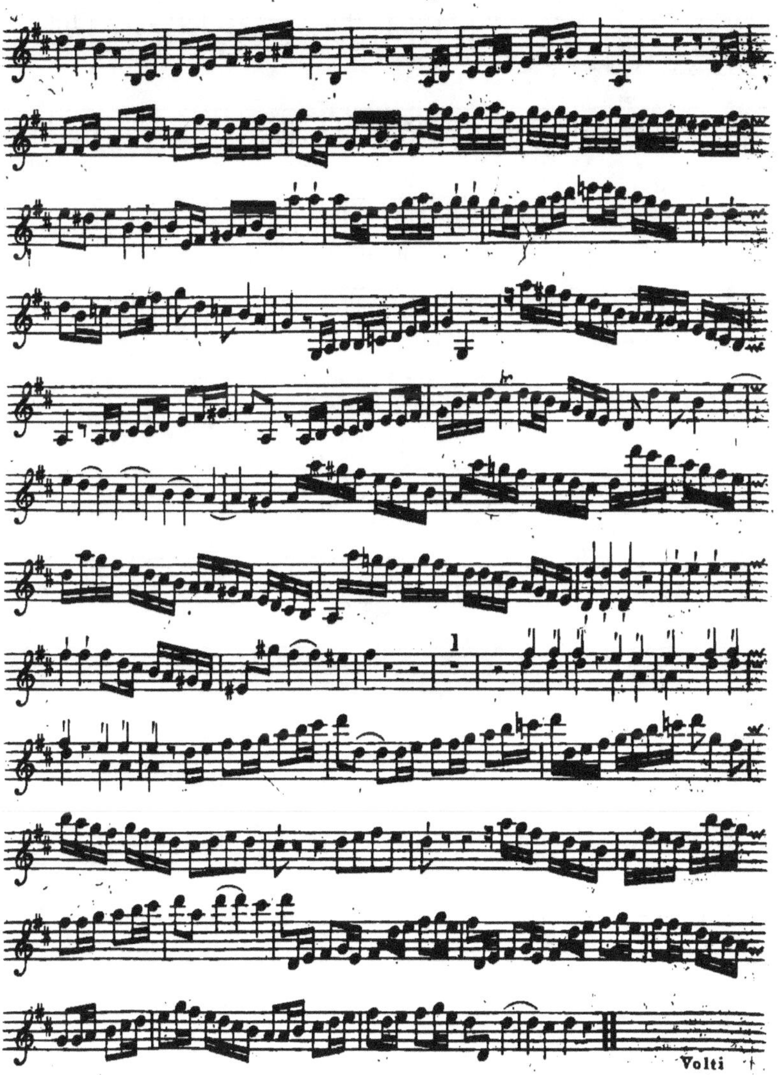

Volti

VIOLINO SECONDO RIPIENO

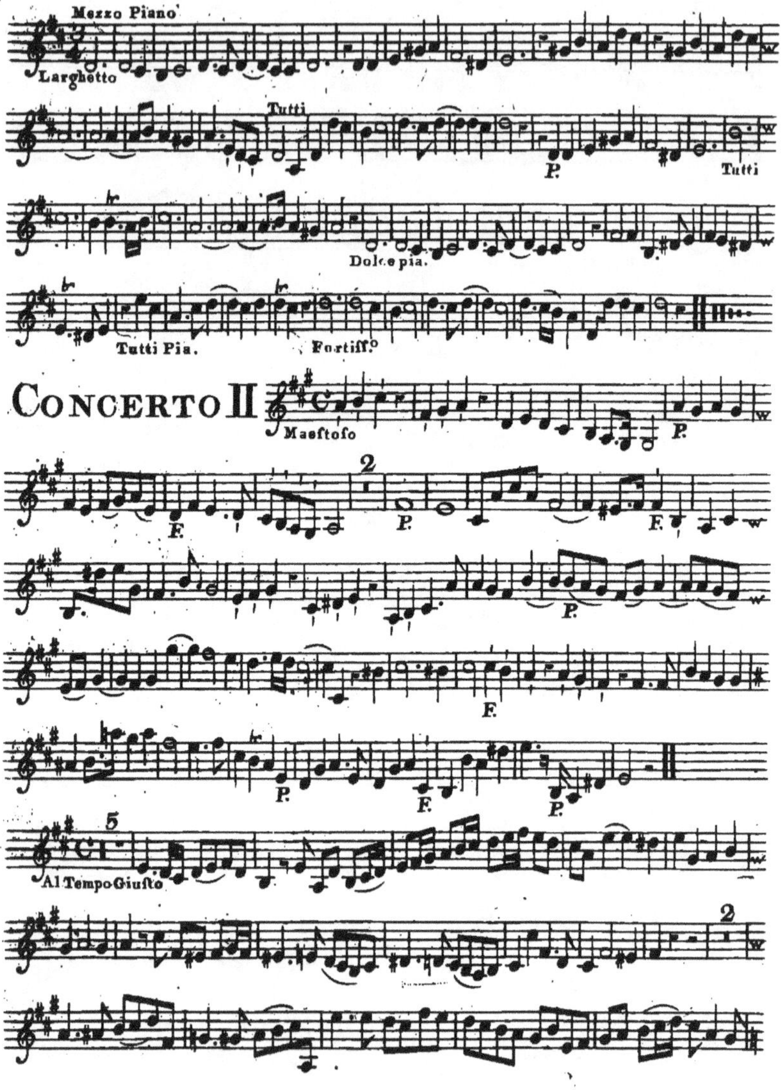

VIOLIN SECONDO RIPIENO

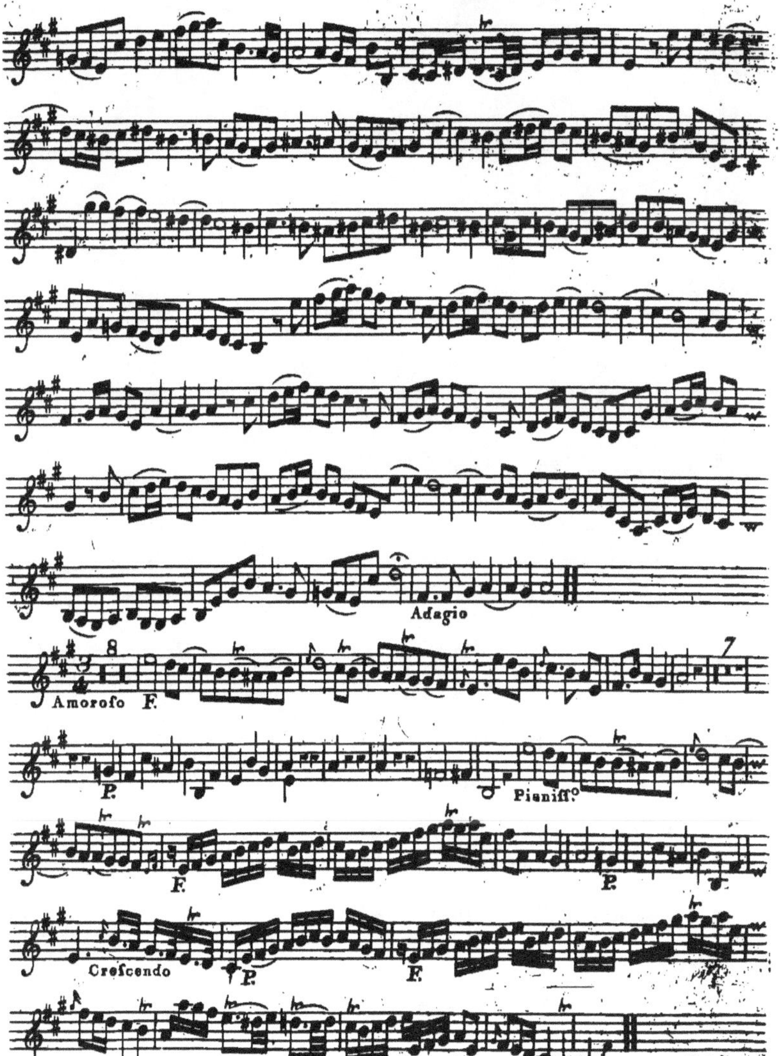

VIOLINO SECONDO RIPIENO

CONCERTO III

Adagio

Allegro

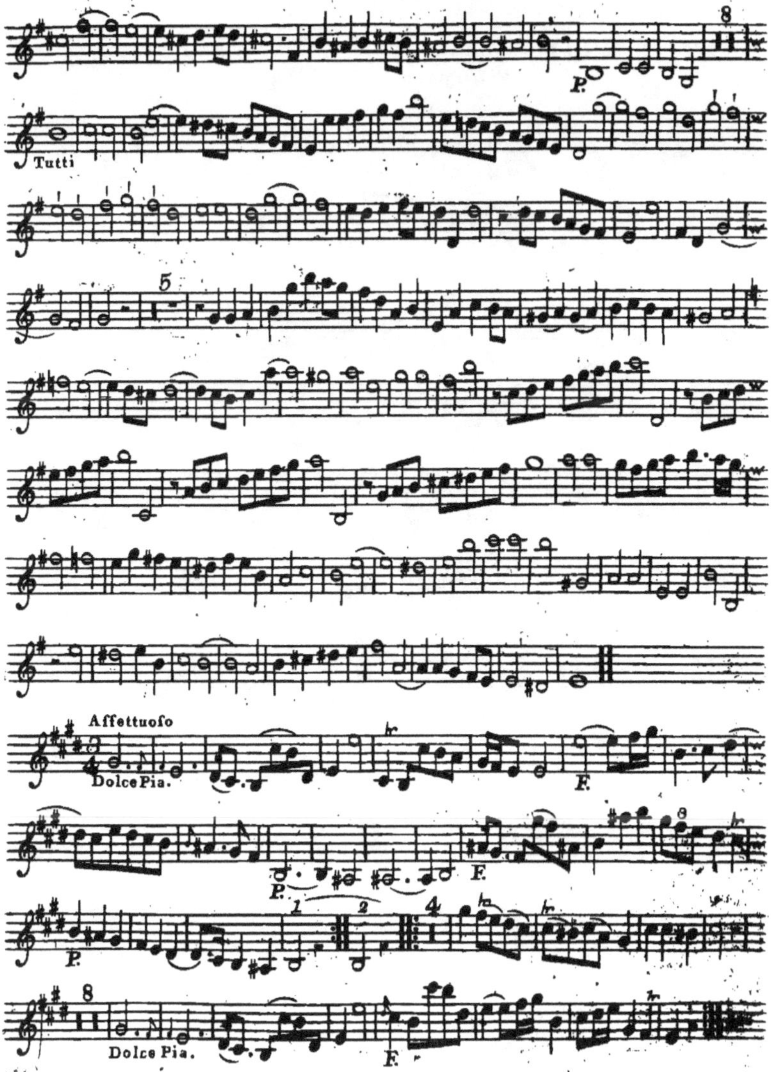
8
P.
Tutti
5
Affettuoso
Dolce Pia.
F.
P.
F.
P.
1
2
4
8
Dolce Pia.
F.

CONCERTO IV

VIOLINO SECONDO RIPIENO

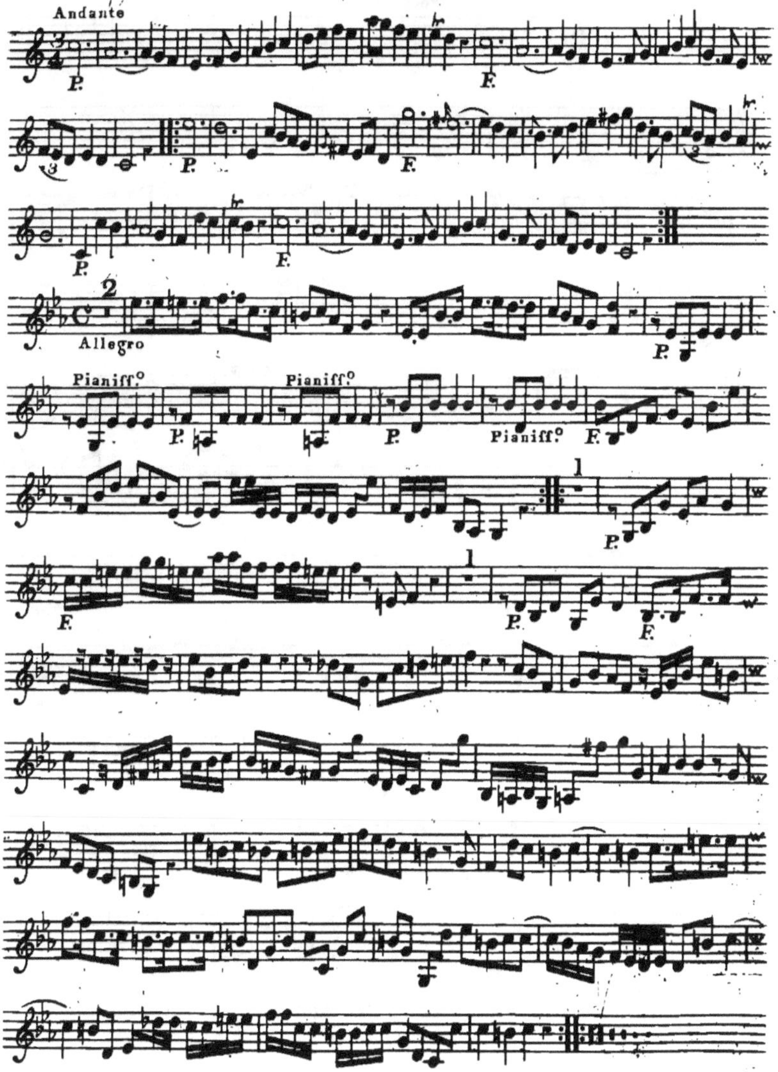

CONCERTO V

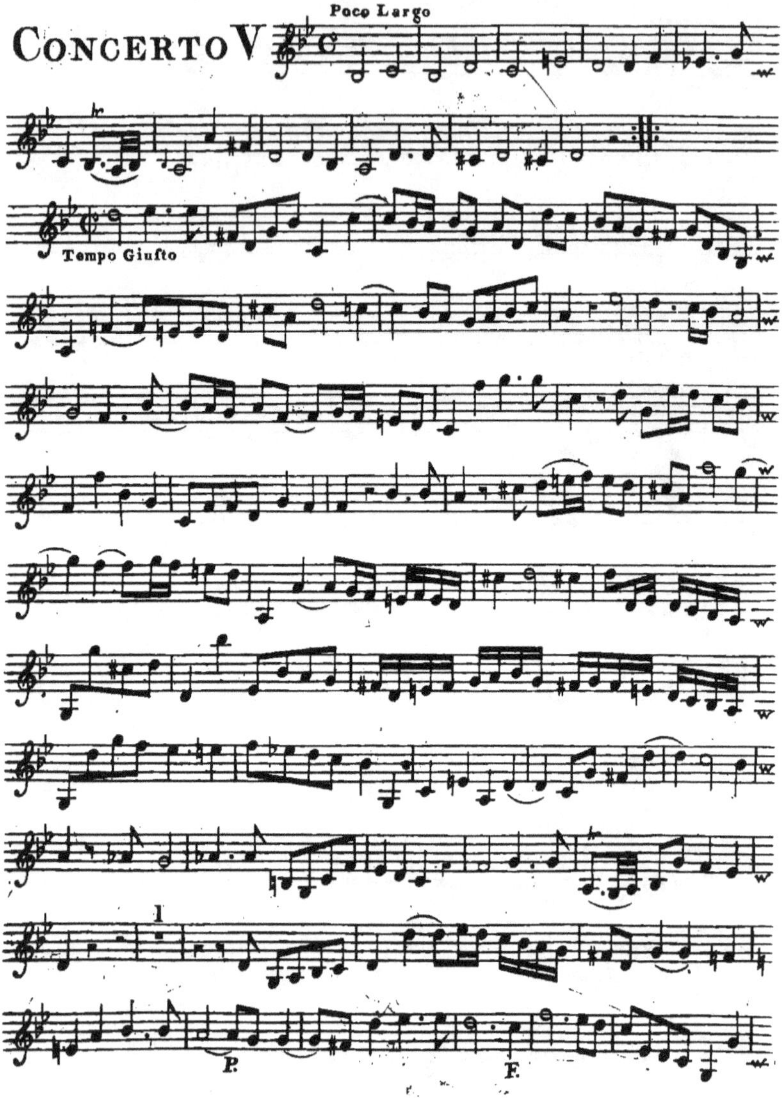

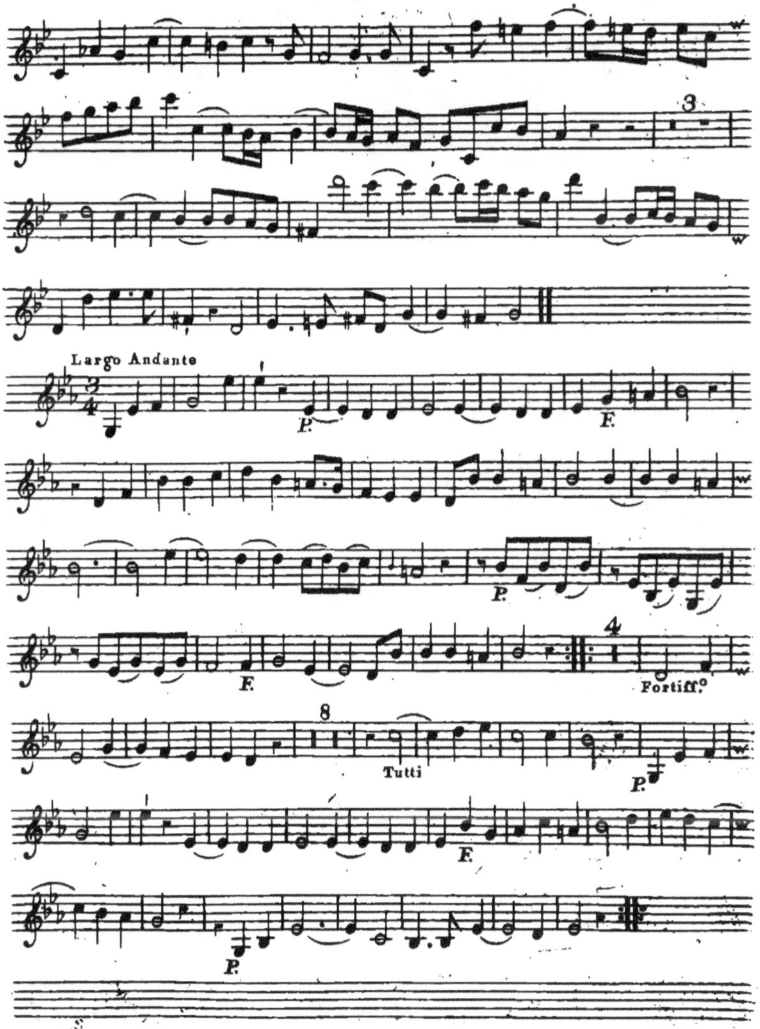

Volti

VIOLINO SECONDO RIPIENO

CONCERTO VI

VIOLINO SECONDO RIPIENO

FOR

FOUR VIOLINS, a TENOR VIOLIN,

A

VIOLONCELLO,

With a THOROUGH BASS for the

HARPSICORD,

Compos'd by

CAPEL BOND,

ORGANIST of COVENTRY.

N. B. The Firſt is for a TRUMPET, the Sixth a BASSOON CONCERTO.

Printed for the Author; and Sold by Mrs. Johnson, *Cheapſide,* London, and by
Mr. Bond at Coventry.
MDCCLXVI.

CONCERTO I

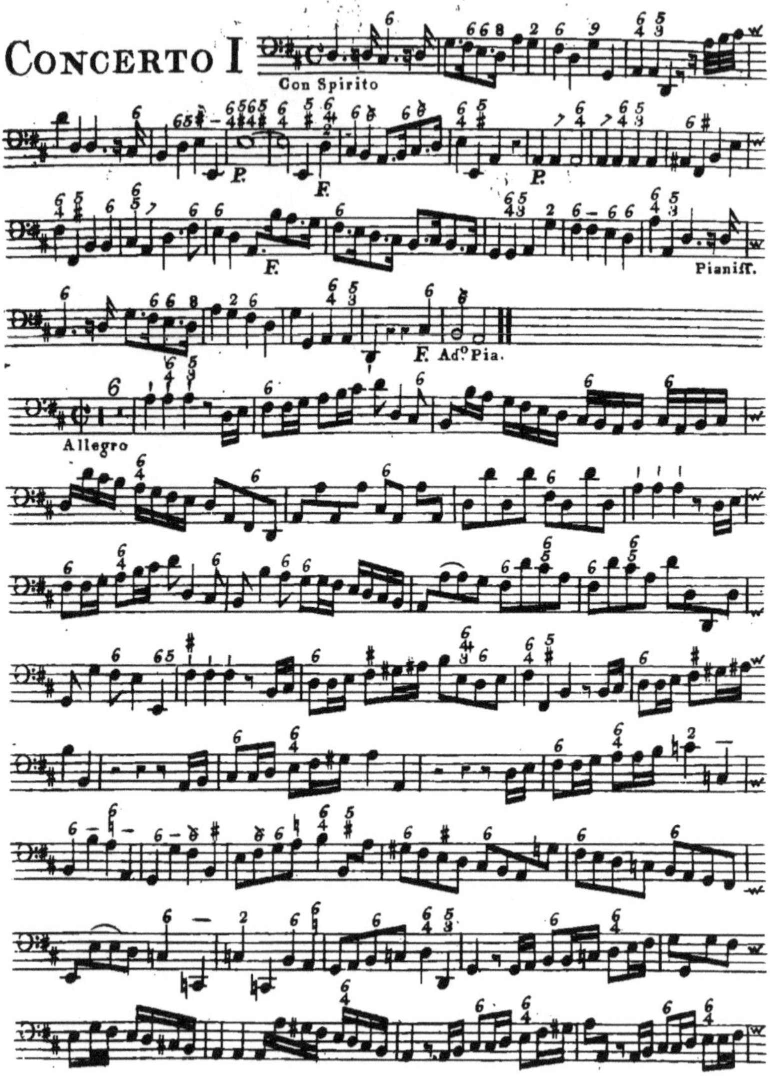
Con Spirito
P.
F.
P.
F.
Pianiss.
F. Ad.o Pia.
Allegro

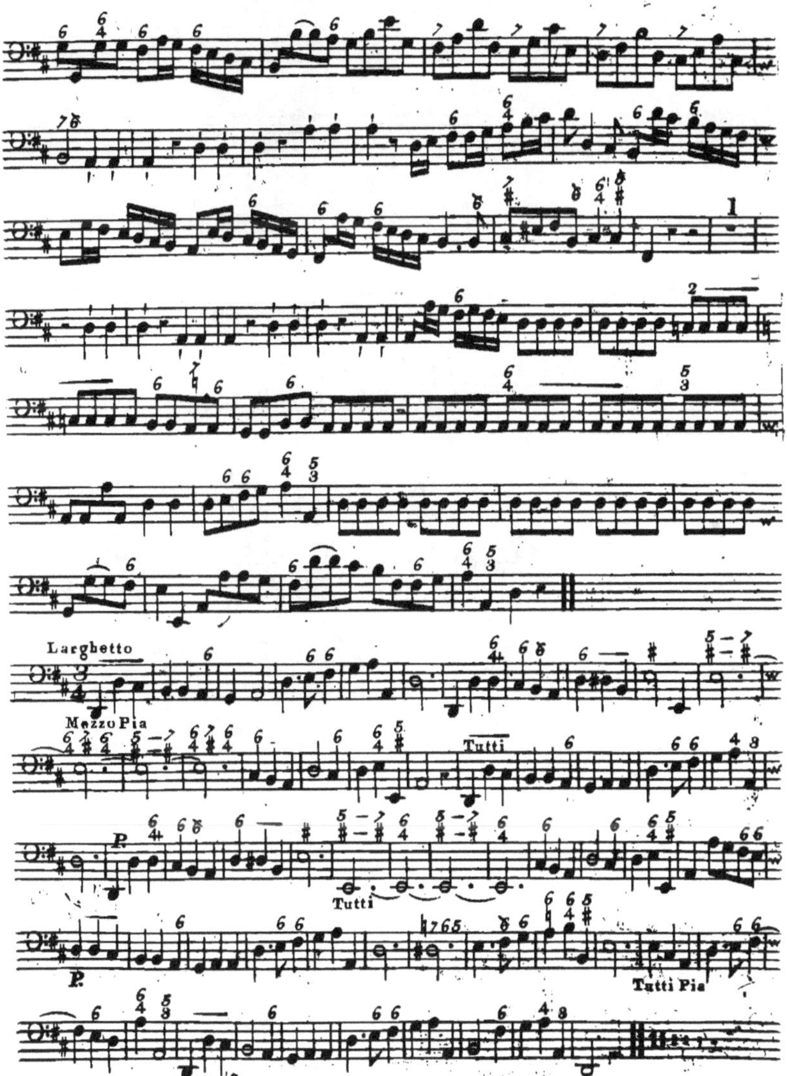
Larghetto
Mezzo Pia
Tutti
P.
Tutti
P.
Tutti Pia
Fortiss.o

CONCERTO II

Maestoso
Pia Violon.
Tutti
P.
F.
P.
Tasto Solo
F.
Pia Tasto Solo
F.
P.
Al Tempo Giusto
Tasto Solo
Adagio

Amoroso
P.
F.
Violon.
Tutti Pia.
Pianiss.º
F.
P.
F.
Violon.
Tutti
Violon. Tutti
Violon.
Tutti
Violon.
Tutti
Violon. Tutti Violon. Tutti
Violon.
Tutti

CONCERTO III

Affettuofo

Dolce Pia.

Soli

Tutti

Soli

Dolce Pia

CONCERTO IV

Larghetto

Ad: Pia   Volti

VIOLONCELLO DEL CONCERTINO

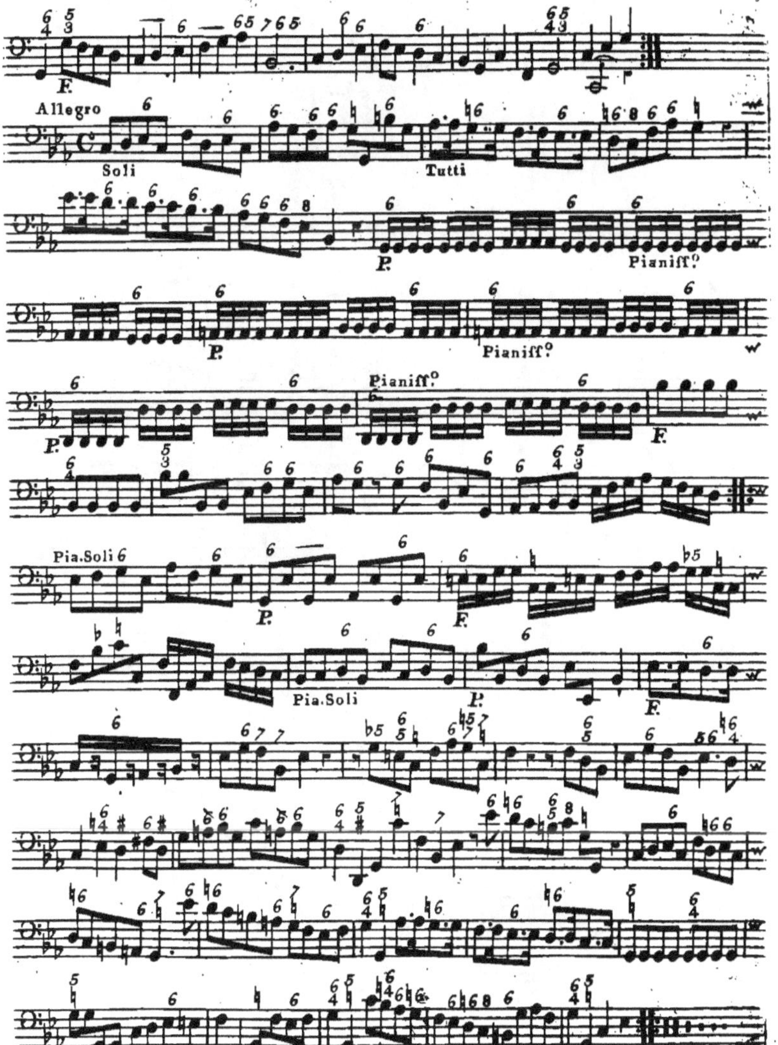
F.
Allegro
Soli
Tutti
P.
Pianiss.°
Pia.Soli

CONCERTO V

Poco Largo

Tempo Giusto

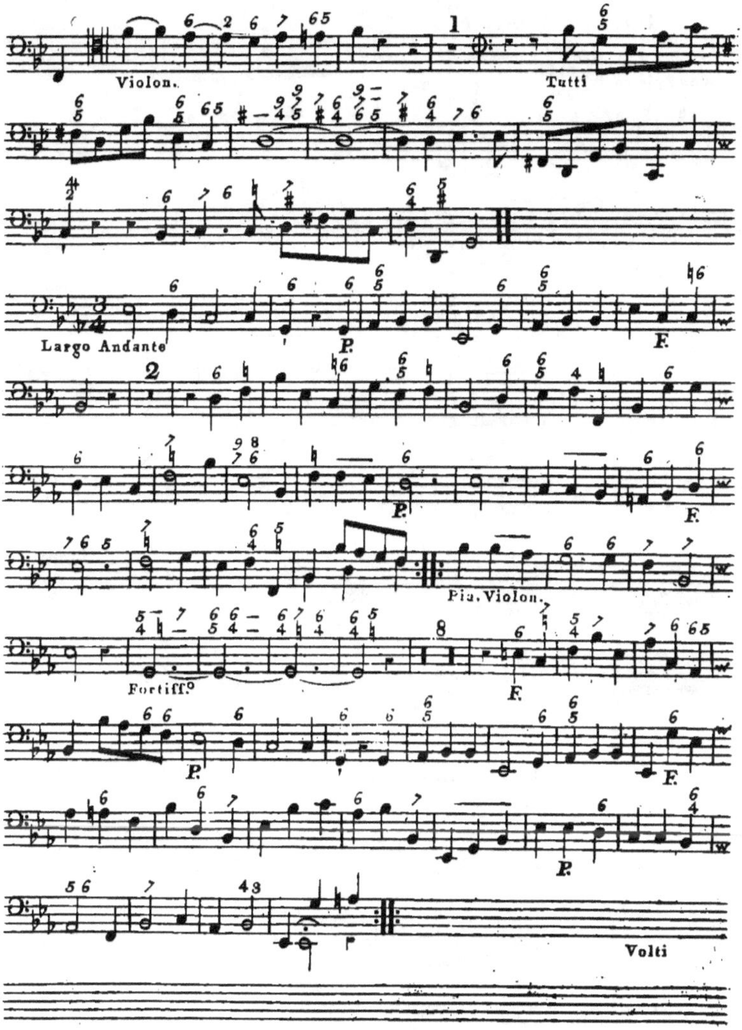
Violon.
Tutti
Largo Andante
P.
F.
Pia. Violon.
Fortiff.o
Volti

VIOLONCELLO DEL CONCERTINO

CONCERTO VI

Andante

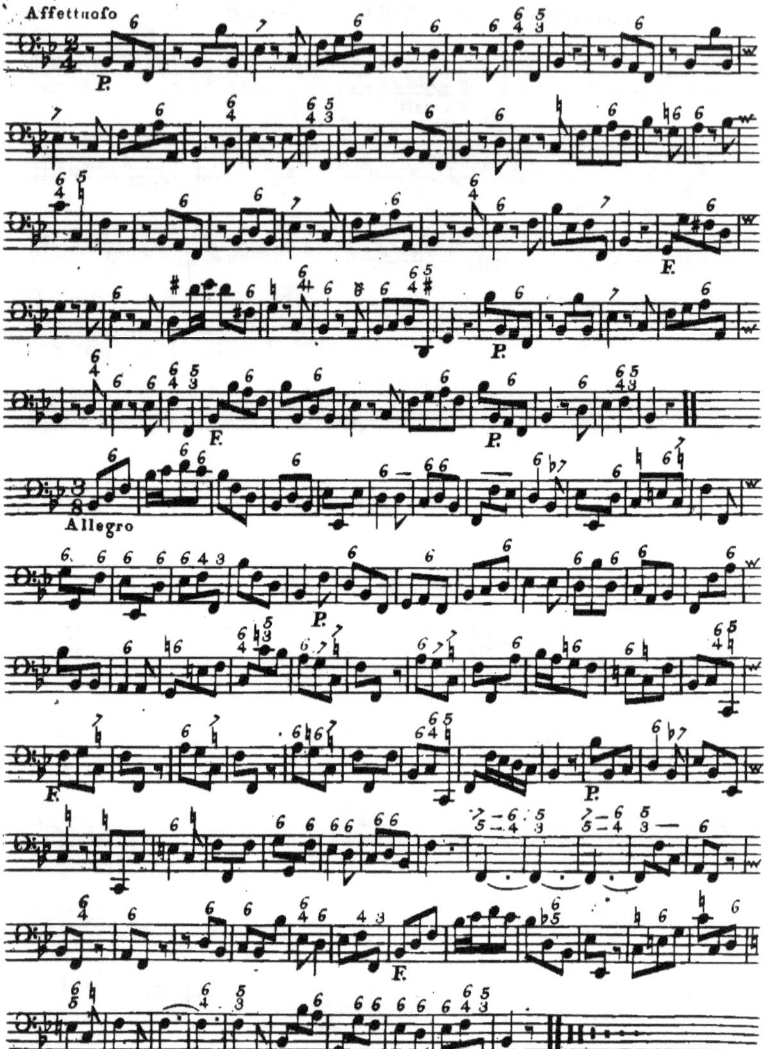
Affettuoso
Allegro

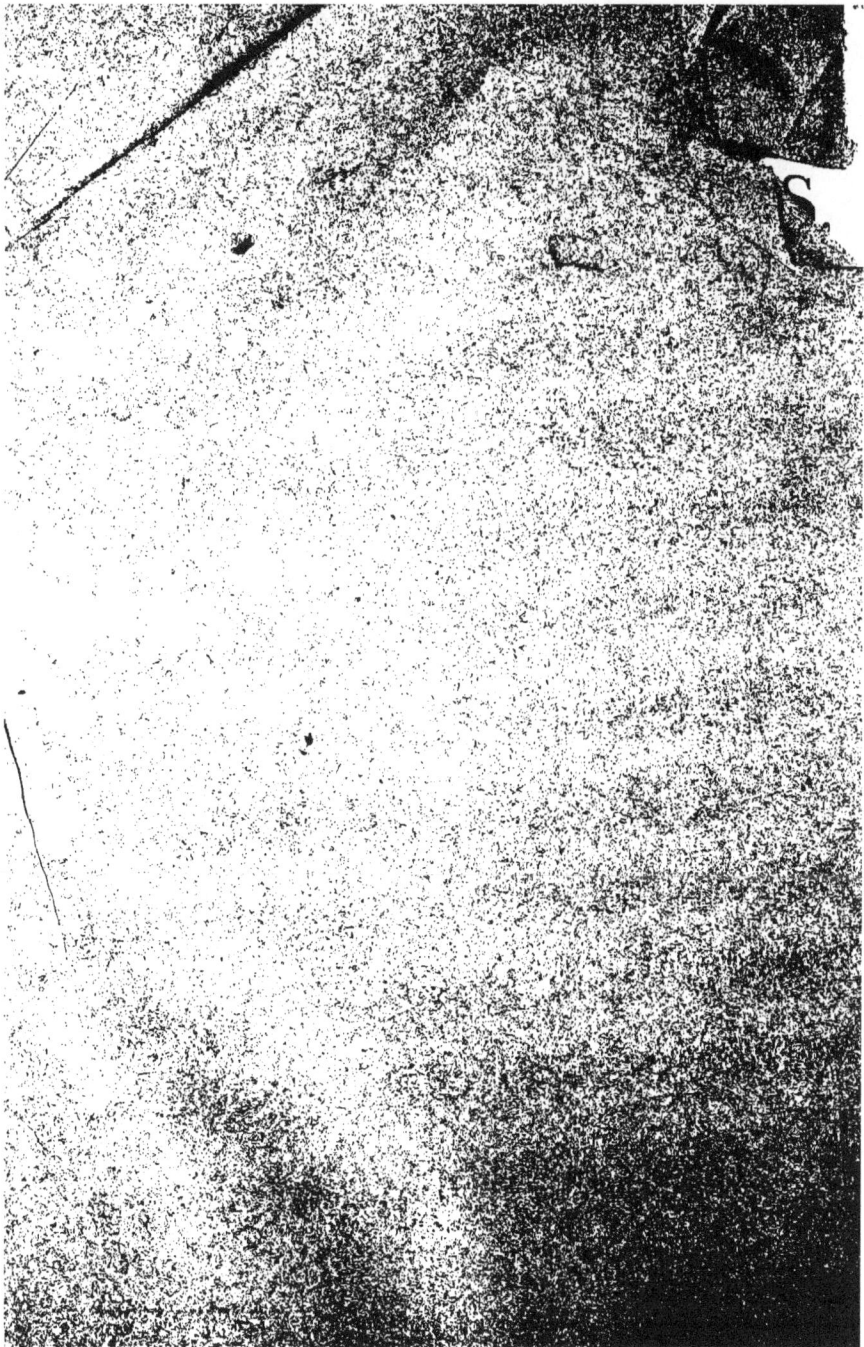

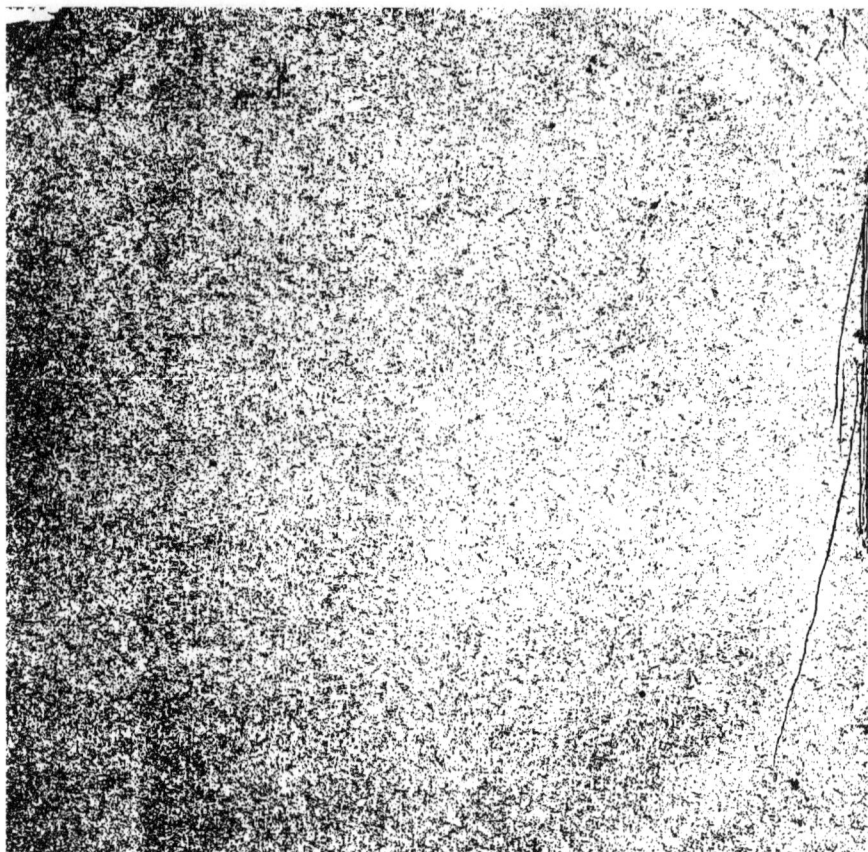

S I X
C O N C E R T O S,

I N

S E V E N   P A R T S,

F O R

FOUR VIOLINS, a TENOR VIOLIN,

A

V I O L O N C E L L O,

With a THOROUGH BASS for the

H A R P S I C O R D,

Compos'd by

C A P E L   B O N D,

O R G A N I S T of C O V E N T R Y.

N. B. The Firſt is for a TRUMPET, the Sixth a BASSOON CONCERTO.

✶✢✳✢✳✢✳✢✳✢✢✳✢✳✢✳✢✳✢✳✢✳✢✳✢✳✢✳✢✳✢✳✢✳✢✳✳

Printed for the Author; and Sold by Mrs. Johnson, *Cheapſide*, London, and by
Mr. Bond at Coventry.
MDCCLXVI.

BASSO RIPIENO

CONCERTO I

Larghetto

Mezzo Pia.

Tutti

P.

Tutti Pia. Fortiff.º

CONCERTO II

Maeftofo

TaftoSolo

Pia.TaftoSolo F. P. Volti

Basso Ripieno

Al Tempo Giuſto

Taſto Solo

Adagio

Amoroſo

Tutti Pia.

Pianiff.º

CONCERTO III

BASSO RIPIENO

CONCERTO IV

Larghetto
P.
F.
Adº Pia.
Tempo Giusto
Tasto Solo
Adº
Andante
Volti.

BASSO RIPIENO

CONCERTO V

Poco Largo

Tempo Giusto

Largo Andante

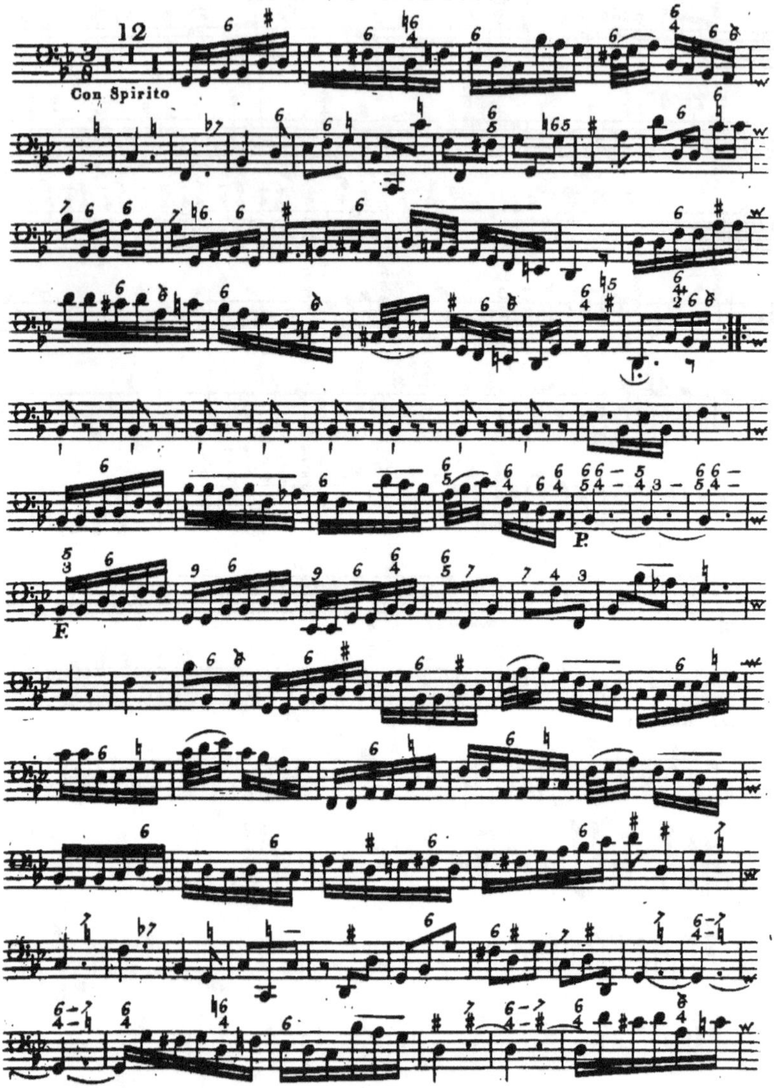
12
Con Spirito
P.
F.

CONCERTO VI

Andante

Volti

BASSO RIPIENO

SIX
CONCERTOS,

IN

SEVEN PARTS,

FOR

FOUR VIOLINS, a TENOR VIOLIN,

A

VIOLONCELLO,

With a THOROUGH BASS for the

HARPSICORD,

Compos'd by

CAPEL BOND,

ORGANIST of COVENTRY.

N. B. The Firſt is for a TRUMPET, the Sixth a BASSOON CONCERTO.

Printed for the Author; and Sold by Mrs. Johnson, *Cheapſide*, London, and by Mr. Bond at Coventry.
MDCCLXVI.

CONCERTO I

Con Spirito

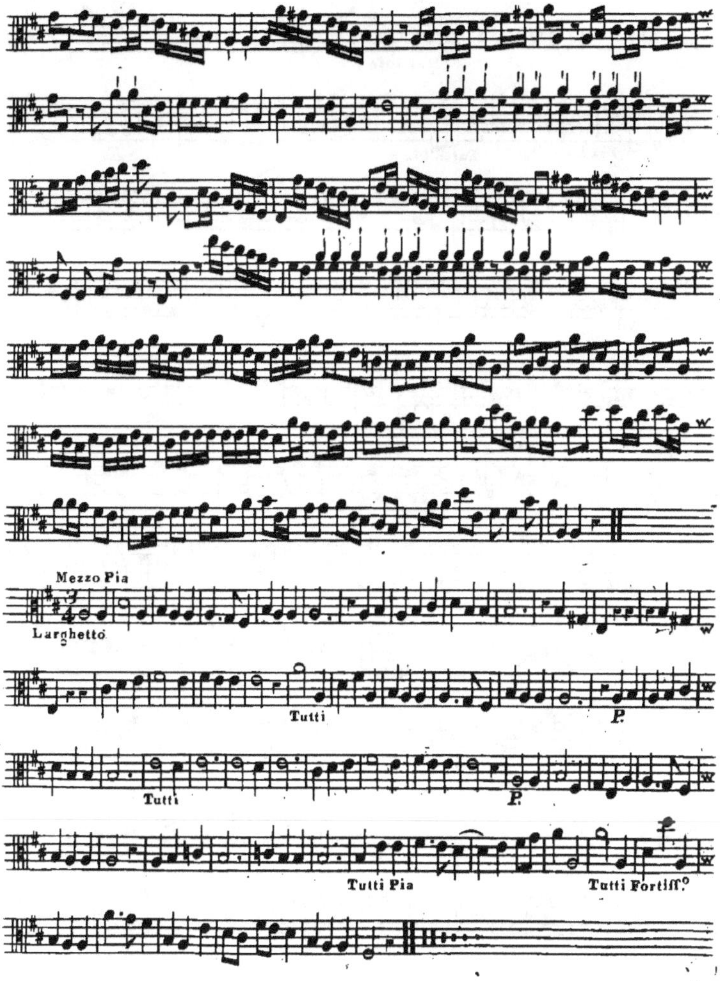
Mezzo Pia
Larghetto
Tutti
P.
Tutti
P.
Tutti Pia
Tutti Fortiss°

CONCERTO II

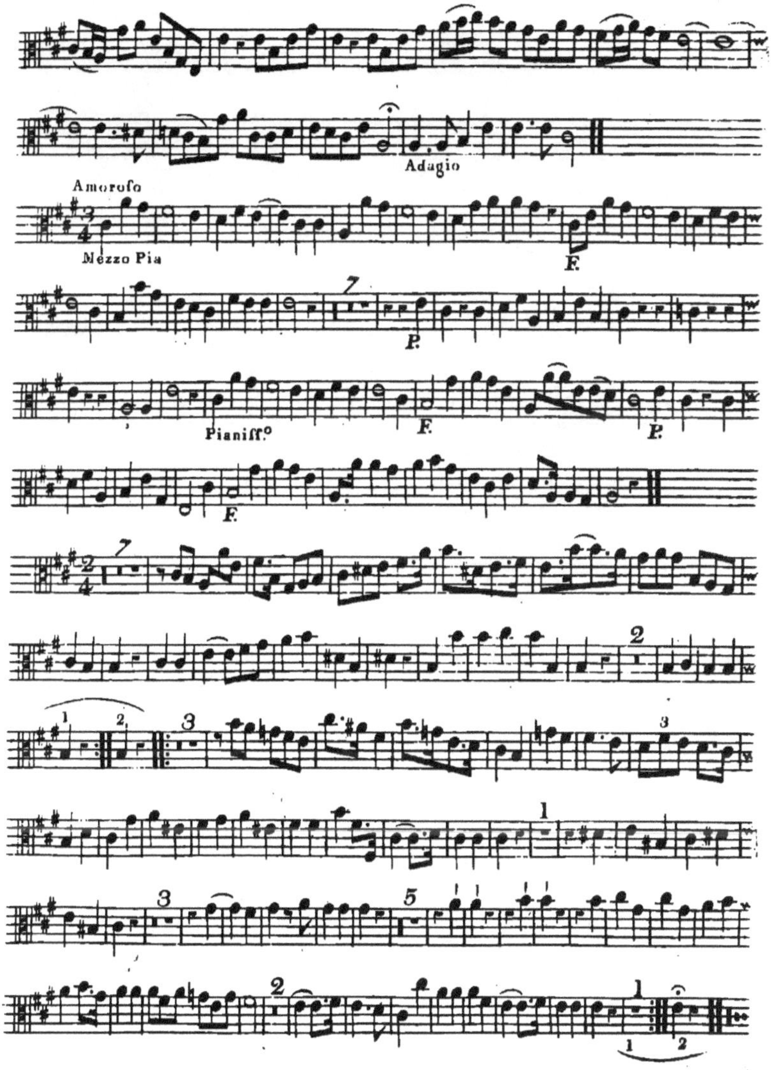
Adagio
Amorofo
Mezzo Pia
F.
P.
Pianiff.o
F.
P.
F.

CONCERTO III

Affettuofo

Dolce Pia

CONCERTO IV — Larghetto

Tempo Giufto

Adg⁰   Volti

ALTO VIOLA

P.
Andante
F.
P.
F.
P.
F.
2
Allegro
Pia.
Pianiss?
Pia.
Pianiss?
Pia.
Pianiss?
1
P.
F.
1
P.
F.

CONCERTO V

Poco Largo

Tempo Giusto

Volti

Largo Andante   P.   F.

Fortiff.°   P.

F.   P.

F.   P.

10
Con Spirito

P.   F.

CONCERTO VI

Andante

ALTO VIOLA

SLOW
P.
Affettuoso
7
P.
Crescendo
Pianiss.
Crescendo
F.
6
Crescendo
F.
P.
tr
Allegro
18
4
P.
15
F.

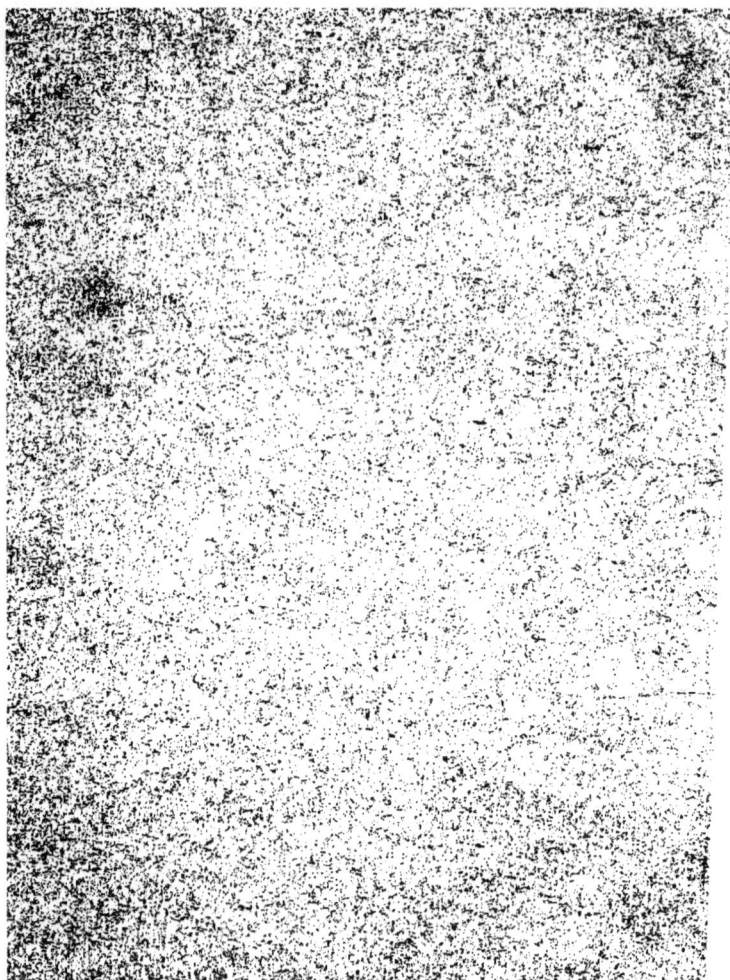

SIX
CONCERTOS,

IN

SEVEN PARTS,

FOR

FOUR VIOLINS, a TENOR VIOLIN,

A

VIOLONCELLO,

With a THOROUGH BASS for the

HARPSICORD,

Compos'd by

CAPEL BOND,

ORGANIST of COVENTRY.

N. B. The Firſt is for a TRUMPET, the Sixth a BASSOON CONCERTO.

Printed for the AUTHOR; and Sold by Mrs. JOHNSON, *Cheapſide,* LONDON, and by
Mr. BOND at COVENTRY.
MDCCLXVI.

CONCERTO I

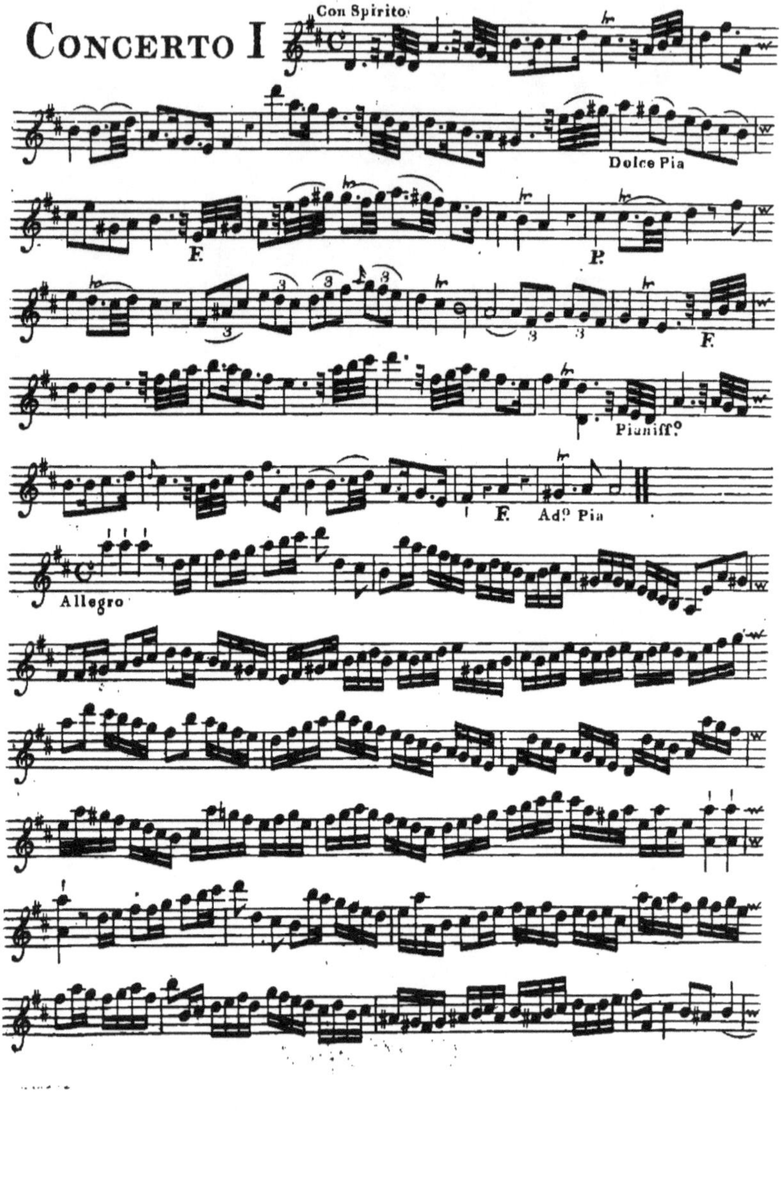

Volti

VIOLINO PRIMO RIPIENO

CONCERTO II

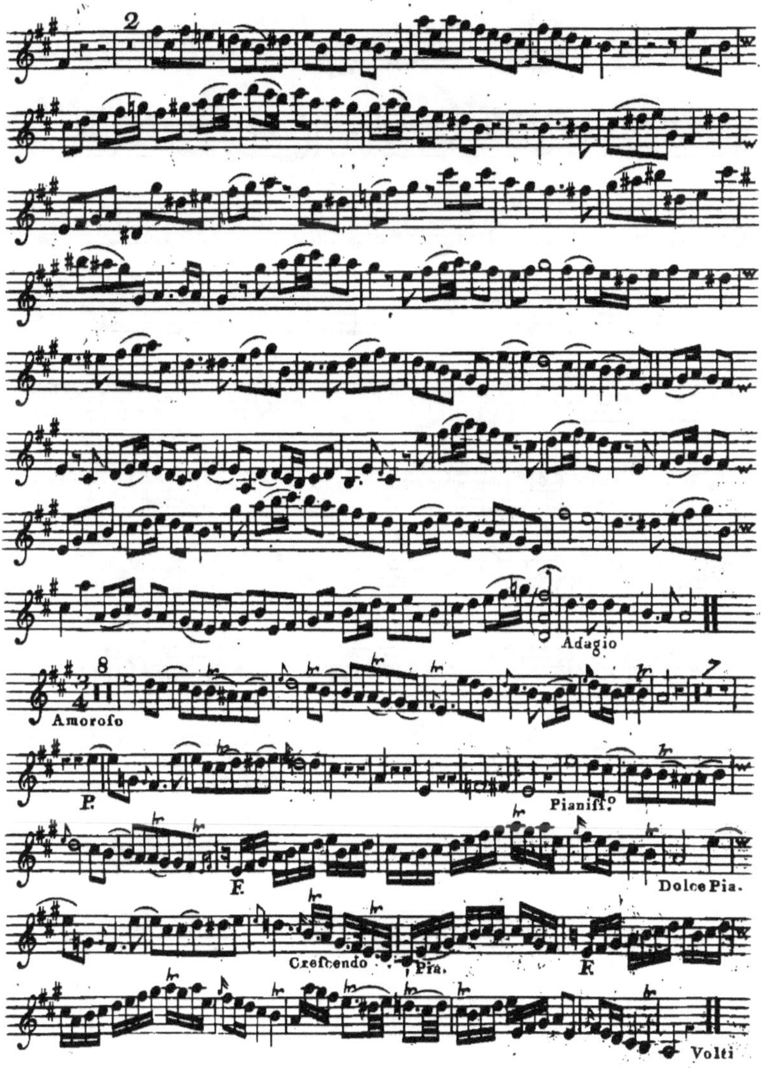
Adagio
Amoroso
P.
Pianiss.°
F.
Dolce Pia.
Crescendo
Pia.
F
Volti

CONCERTO III

Adagio

Allegro

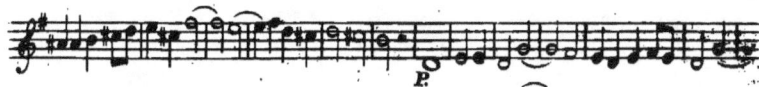

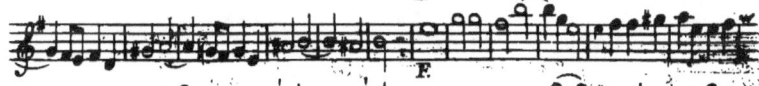

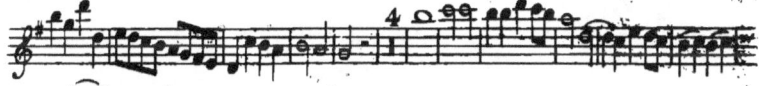

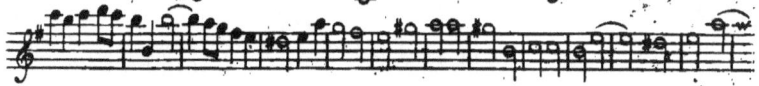

VIOLINO PRIMO RIPIENO

Andante
P.
F.
P.
F.
P.
F.
2
Allegro
P.
Pianiss.o
P.
Pianiss.
P.
Pianiss.o
F.
1
P.
F.
1
P.
F.

CONCERTO V

Poco Largo

Tempo Giusto

Tutti

P.

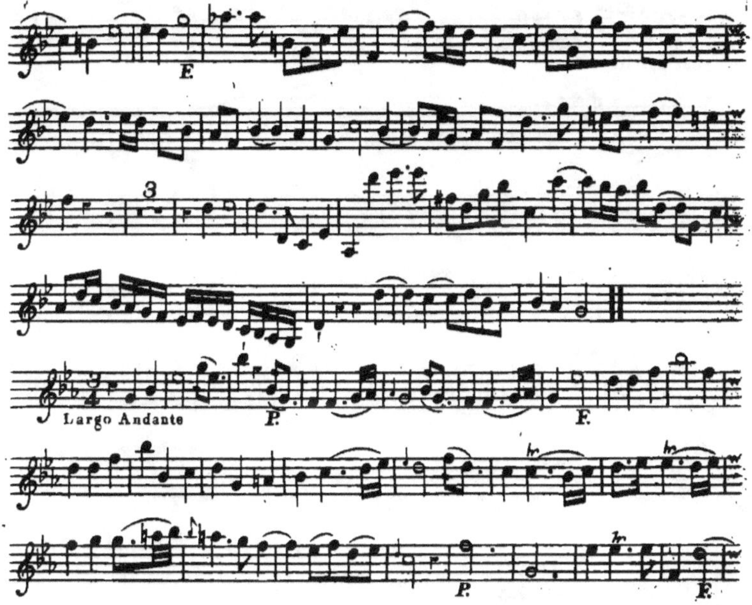
3
Largo Andante
P.
F.
P.
F.
3
8
F.
P.
F.
1
P.
Volti

VIOLINO PRIMO RIPIENO

Con Spirito

CONCERTO VI

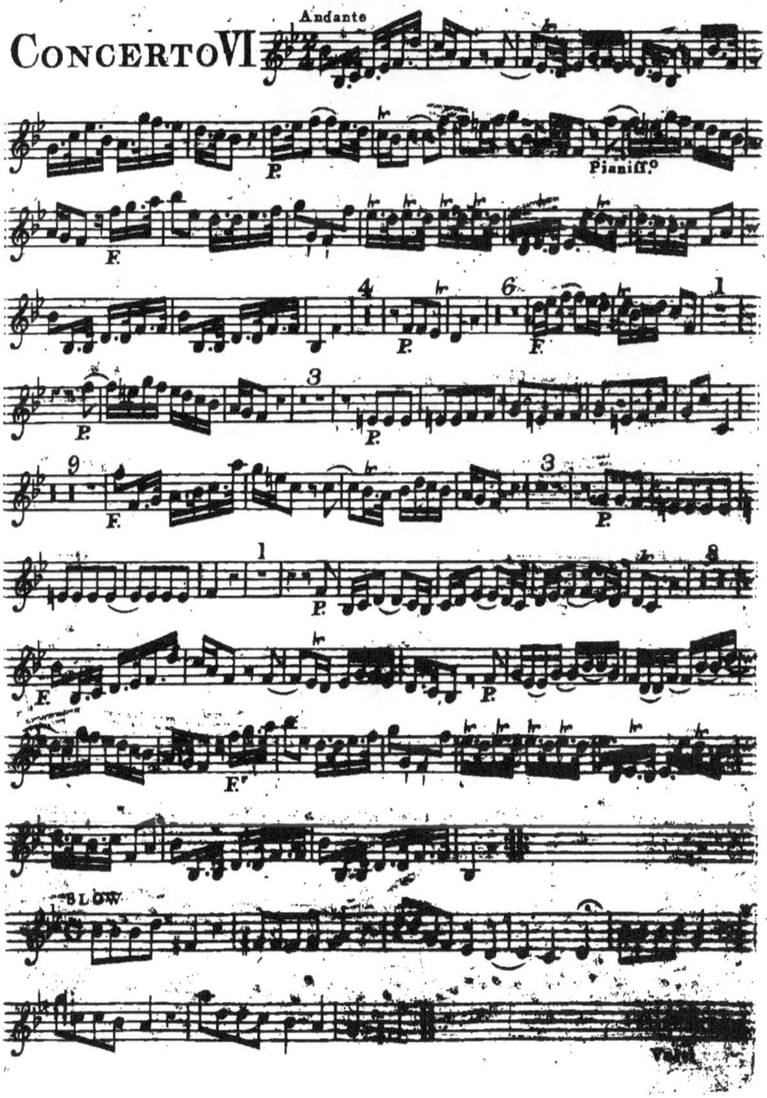

VIOLINO PRIMO RIPIENO

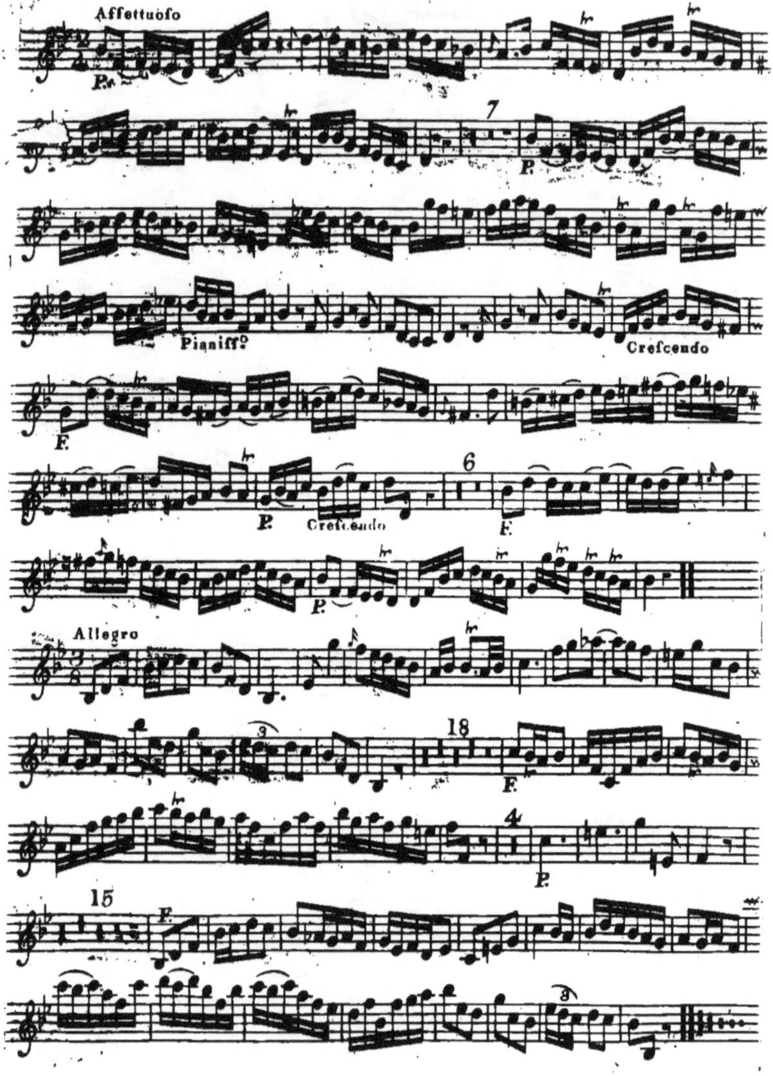